Horse Trails of "Colorful" Colorado
Central Colorado — Book 2

(Contains trails from Adams, Boulder, Douglas and Jefferson Counties)

D1608768

**28 Trails with Pictures & Information of Importance
For
Horseback Riders**

By
Janet M. St. Jacques

Horse Trails of "Colorful" Colorado
Central Colorado– Book 2

Copyright ©2005 by "Ride The Western Trails Publications"

Published by: Ride The Western Trails Publications
2204 Eagle Drive, Loveland, CO   80537

First Edition

ISBN 0-9763431-1-8

"A good man is concerned for the welfare of his animals."

The Lord says: "I will guide you along the best pathway for your life. I will advise you and watch over you."

Proverbs 12:10

Psalm 32:8

Table of Contents

Foreword

Looking back since the release of my first book, Northern Colorado – Book 1, it's hard for me to grasp that a whole year has passed. I've used this time to research new trails, ride the trails I chose for this book, update my camera and software, attend conferences and meet some very interesting people. I took all of the comments I received on Book 1 and did my best to improve on Book 2. Central Colorado Book 2 has six additional trails with even more pictures to increase the book by over a hundred pages!! Also included are various horse quotes that I have placed at the end of every map that I hope you enjoy reading as much as I do. Again, I tried to include trails for all levels of riders and horses as well as incorporate trails that can be ridden year round. One of my biggest discoveries was that traveling south from Loveland with my horse trailer was just as easy as traveling north from Loveland. This has been a year of growth for me and "Gem" and has me "chomping at the bit" to see what the next year will bring!

<u>Disclaimer</u>

Horseback riding can be dangerous even when riding a well trained horse with an experienced rider. Information contained within these pages has been gathered from many sources. At publication, every effort was made to ensure the accuracy of the information. Even though I used a GPS unit, its coverage - as well as cell phone coverage - was at times intermittent. This information is published for general reference and not as a substitute for independent verification by users when circumstances warrant. The author, Janet St. Jacques, sponsors, advertisers and/or anyone contributing information to this book will not be held responsible for any inconvenience or injury resulting from the use or misuse of the maps, diagrams or text contained within this book.

Definition of "Difficulty" Rating

EASY: These trails are great for the beginning trail rider or inexperienced horse. Elevation is gradual and minimal. The trail has no obstacles and footing is good.

MODERATE: These trails are for the rider or horse that has completed several trail rides. There are some obstacles (easy-to-cross bridges, slow moving, shallow water crossing, etc.) and/or steeper climbs. The footing may have a few rocky spots and/or narrow paths.

DIFFICULT: These trails are strenuous for both the rider and the horse. There are many obstacles (bridges may be narrow and high above the ground, water may be fast moving and deep, etc.) and/or very steep climbs. The footing may be very rocky and there may be portions of the trail where you need to get off your horse and walk. The trail itself may be very long. These trails need an experienced rider and a well conditioned, well trained, experienced trail horse. If you are "curling your toes" in your boots, you know that you are on a difficult section of the trail.

Trail Etiquette

❖ Park in such a way as not to block anyone else in.
❖ Be considerate if space is limited and park so others will have room to park.
❖ Say "hello" to the people you meet on the trails. We need to share trails and spreading good will among other trail users can help avoid potential conflict.
❖ Bicyclers yield to hikers and horses. Hikers yield to horses.

❖ Downhill trail users must "always" yield to uphill trail users.
❖ Stay on the trails to avoid and not disturb wildlife. If you need to move off the trail, ride within 10 feet of the trail. You may ride beyond the 10 feet limit briefly to avoid imminent danger to other persons.
❖ Approach turns in anticipation of someone around the bend.
❖ Be prepared for the unexpected by being aware of what is going on around you. A horse does not take time to reason, they react by instinct.
❖ If your horse is a kicker, put a red ribbon on its tail as a warning. Remember, you are responsible for controlling your horse on the trail.
❖ When you need to pass someone on the trail, call out "passing on your left" to warn them.

Trail Etiquette
(Continued)

- ❖ If you are being passed, pull off to the right and try to have your horse face the trail. Do not turn the horse so that they have to pass his/her rear end and risk being kicked.
- ❖ Remember the gate rule – if a gate is open, leave it open – if a gate is closed, close it after you ride through.
- ❖ Carry out all trash. Try to leave your camp and trails even cleaner than when you found them.
- ❖ Don't ride and drink alcohol. You need your best judgment to ride and handle your horse through trail obstacles.
- ❖ Do not clean out your horse trailer of manure and/or wood shavings at the parking lot. Even though manure is totally bio-degradable, keep the parking area as clean as possible by moving and scattering any manure off to the grassy area. Don't leave the impression to other trail users that horses "litter."
- ❖ During hunting season, wear plenty of hunter orange on yourself as well as on your horse.

General Location Map
(This map is for reference only; the map is NOT to scale)

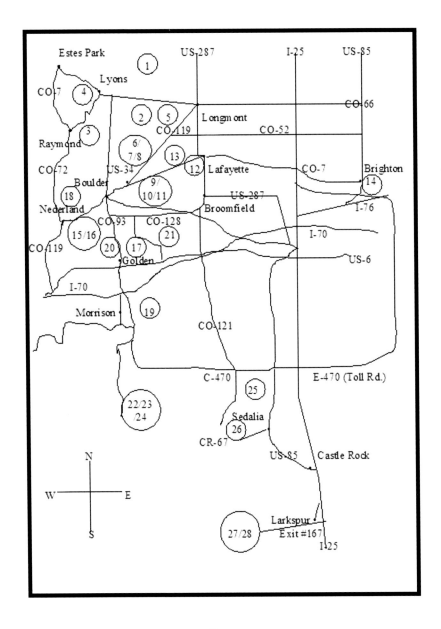

Trail # 1

Trail Name:

Rabbit Mountain (Boulder)

Govt. Organization: Boulder County Parks and Open Lands

Fees: None

Beginning Elevation: 5,500 ft.

Ending Elevation: 5,850 ft. (The Loop) or 6,000 ft. (The Overlook)

Trailer Parking: Four designated spots for horse trailers

Facilities: Restrooms are available at the trailhead as well as picnic facilities. For information on a group shelter that can accommodate 30 people call (303) 441-4557. This is a "dry" trail, water is not available.

Difficulty: Easy to Moderate. Portions of the route are rocky with minimal space for passing others on the trail.

Length of Trail: Approximately 7.6 miles roundtrip – Eagle Wind Trail (3 miles loop), the Little Thompson Overlook Trail (2 miles roundtrip) and the Indian Mesa Trail (2.6 miles roundtrip)

Trail Usage: Horseback riding, hiking, biking
Dogs are permitted on leash.

Directions: From I 25, turn west on Exit #243 (Ute Hwy/CO 66) and travel approximately 7 miles. From the intersection of US 287 and CO 66 in north Longmont, continue west 6.8 miles to North 53rd Street. Turn north just past the Longmont Water Tank and follow the road 2.8 miles to the trailhead.

Entrance to Rabbit Mountain parking area

Designated horse trailer parking

Restrooms at the trailhead

Group picnic area at the trailhead

Watch out for this sharp edge at the Kiosk

Trail leaving the trailhead, easy ride

Starting a gradual climb and the trail becomes a little rockier

Service Road parallels the first section of the trail

Turn off for the Little Thompson Overlook Trail, the Indian Mesa Trail and the Eagle Wind Trail

Heading up the Eagle Wind Trail

View from Eagle Wind Trail

Eagle Wind Trail does a loop here

Trail becomes wooded and rocky

Up to $300 fine if found riding in this restricted area

Trail can become very rocky; shoes are a must

Taking the Service Road on the return to the trailhead

Trail veers from the Service Road to continue to the trailhead

Another rider we met on the trail "ponying"

General Information: The Rabbit Mountain Open space trails are well maintained, marked with sign posts and easy to follow. Bridges, water crossings and other obstacles that I would consider to be difficult riding are missing here. Shoes are a must if you ride the Little Thompson Overlook Trail or the Eagle Wind Trail. Shoes are not needed if you stay on the Service Road and the Indian Mesa trail.

Leaving from the trailhead, watch out for the roof of the Kiosk that is located right next to the trail. If your horse is spooky, I would walk my horse and mount only after I had passed it. From here you have the choice of following the trail or riding a little east and connecting to the Service Road. Being that the Service Road is an easy ride, we usually leave it for the return trip. At approximately .5 mile into the ride, the trail forks off to the various trails. The Little Thompson Overlook Trail uses the dirt road for .3 miles and then breaks off to the west. The path becomes very rocky and steep for the remaining .5 miles, coming to a dead end with a beautiful view. This rocky trail is used more by hikers and cyclists. The Indian Mesa Trail follows a road east for a short way before turning north to the boundary of the park. This is a very easy ride and would be good for a green horse or a green rider. I have met very few hikers or bicycles on this trail. The Eagle Wind Trail is the most popular trail for the equestrian. It is also well-liked by the hikers and bicyclists. There are a few locations where the space is limited if meeting other users on the trail. This route is also rocky but not as difficult as the Little Thompson Overlook Trail. You will eventually come to a point where the trail loops. At this "Y," we usually take the trail to the right, as do most other users of this trail. Take the time to stop and take in the views. Riding is "side-by-side" on the Indian Mesa Trail and the Service Road, otherwise ride "head-to-tail."

Watch for rattle snakes and the occasional mountain lion. I've ridden here year round, but check in the winter for snow on the trails. In the summer, hats, sunglasses and sun block are a must.

Notes:

Map:

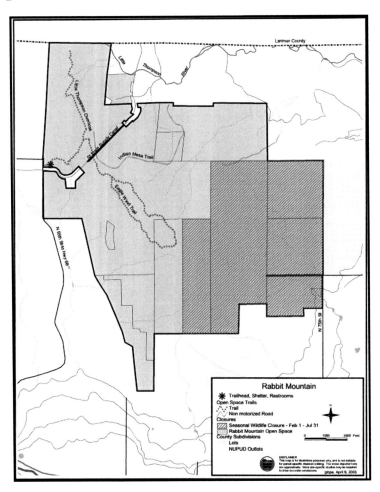

National Geographic Map #100

"A pony is a childhood dream. A horse is an adult treasure."
–Rebecca Carroll

Trail #2
Trail Name:

Pella Crossing (Boulder)

Govt. Organization: Boulder County Parks and Open Lands

Fees: None

Beginning Elevation: 5,110 ft.

Ending Elevation: 5,110 ft.

Trailer Parking: Designated area for trailers. Ample room to maneuver

Facilities: Restrooms are available at the trailhead as well as picnic facilities. For information on a group shelter that can accommodate 30 people call (303) 441-4557. This is a "dry" trail, water is not available.

Difficulty: Easy (Complete your ride before 6 PM to avoid a train that passes)

Length of Trail: Approximately 3 miles round trip (Braly Trails, 2 miles – Marlatt Trails – 1 mile)

Trail Usage: Horseback riding, hiking, biking
Dogs are permitted on a leash.

Directions: From I 25, turn west on Exit #243 (Ute Hwy/CO 66). Drive west approximately 10.5 miles on CO 66 to 75th Street. Travel south on 75th Street 1.0 mile to Hygiene Road. Park is 1/4 mile south of Hygiene Road & 75th Street on the east (left hand) side.

Entrance to Pella Crossing

Parking area, park along the north end

Restroom facilities at Braly Trails, Port-a-potty at Marlatt Trails

Take the right trail at fork toward Webster Pond

Picnic facilities south of the parking lot

Ride to the right around Heron Lake

**Railroad tracks along the north side of Heron Lake
and Sunset Pond**

A trail goes between Heron Lake and Sunset Pond

Back to trailhead or continue to the Marlatt Trails

Cross 75ᵗʰ Street to continue to the Marlatt Trails

Beginning of the Marlatt Trails, notice the RR tracks

Trail passes Dragonfly Pond

Trail loops around Poplar Pond

Dead end if you ride down this trail

General Information: What a find for a winter ride or a green horse and/or green rider! Because of the fine gravel, no shoes are needed. This is a very easy trail that meanders among the various ponds. The trail is fairly wide so that you could ride "side-by-side." Expect to see fisherman with belly-boats as well as people walking their dogs on a leash. Notice that there are railroad tracks that follow the north portion of both trails. According to the locals, a coal train runs daily between 6 PM and 7 PM. Water fowl is abundant in this area, so be aware that your horse may spook to a sudden flight or landing. Noise from small planes as well as car noise from CO 66 was noted. When crossing 75th Street, I would recommend dismounting and walking your horse across. This is not a major road so traffic should be minimal. At the time of this writing, Clearwater Pond was closed for construction, due to open to the public sometime in 2005. Mosquitoes could be a problem in the summer so be sure to protect yourself and your horse. This would be a great place to ride and enjoy a picnic on a nice summer day. I do not believe that this is a heavily used area, so weekend as well as weekday riding could be accommodated.

Notes:

MAP:

National Geographic #100

"In riding a horse, we borrow freedom."
–Helen Thomson

MAP:

National Geographic #100

"No hour of life is lost that is spent in the saddle."
–Winston Churchill

Trail #3
Trail Name:

Heil Valley Ranch (Boulder)

Govt. Organization: Boulder County Parks and Open Lands

Fees: None

Beginning Elevation: 5,668 ft.

Ending Elevation: 6,792 ft.

Trailer Parking: Parking easily accommodates 8 large trailers with ample room to maneuver. Follow signs to the upper parking lot for trailers.

Facilities: At the trailhead, restrooms are available as well as various picnic tables. This is a "dry" trail, water is not available. A group shelter, which can accommodate up to 25 people, is available for use on a first-come, first-serve basis. No groups are permitted on weekends due to limited parking. For reservations, call (303) 441-3950.

Difficulty: Moderate

Length of Trail: Approximately 7.6 miles round trip (Wapiti Trail 5 miles, Ponderosa Loop Trail 2.6 miles)

Trail Usage: Horseback riding, hiking, biking
Dogs are NOT permitted.

Directions: Coming north from Boulder on CO 7/US 36, travel 4.7 miles to Left Hand Canyon Drive. Turn west (left) onto Left Hand Canyon Drive and go 0.7 mile to Geer Canyon Road. Turn north (right) onto Geer Canyon Road (dirt road) traveling through private property 1.3 miles to the trailhead. Heil Ranch parking will be on the right side of the road. Drive to the back, uppermost parking lot for parking your horse trailer.

Trailhead "pull through" parking at the far north parking lot

Restrooms are located by the bottom (south) parking lot

31

Group picnic area

Horses are not permitted on the Lichen Loop

Beginning of trail is wide for "side-by-side" riding

Bells on your horse would be a good idea

Follow Wapiti Trail to the left

The only bridge on the trail you must cross

Various switch backs winding through meadows

Trail meanders through trees and becomes rockier

Remains of a homestead

Service Road, do not enter!!

Continue to Ponderosa Loop

Spectacular view from Ponderosa Loop Trail

General Information: The Heil Valley Ranch consists of 4,923 acres of beautiful backcountry. The beginning of the Wapiti Trail is north of the upper parking lot. The trail starts out narrow for a short distance but will widen allowing for "side-by-side" riding. Continue past Lichen Trail which is clearly marked for pedestrians only. After another short distance the trail will take off to the left (northwest) through an open area. The path will narrow forcing you to ride "head-to tail" for the remaining distance. Ride cautiously through this area, watching for prairie dogs and their burrows. Your next obstacle will be a wooden bridge with high metal sides with a small stream running under it. After crossing the bridge, the trail begins to gain altitude and you will encounter a rockier terrain with switchbacks. Watch for the mule deer as you ride through the pines. Continue to follow the signs for Wapiti Trail, crossing over a Service Road. Shortly after passing the remains of a stone cabin, you will ride up to the beginning of the 2.6 mile Ponderosa Loop Trail. From here you can return on Wapiti Trail (2.5 miles back to the trailhead) or ride Ponderosa Loop Trail (2.6 miles) and then return on Wapiti Trail. The Ponderosa Loop Trail is at the top of the mountain so expect a little elevation gain and spectacular views. Take the time to stop at the vista point on the Loop and take in the landscape.

Be sure to have bells on your horse; bears, mountain lions and bobcats have been sighted in this area. This would be a good trail for your first mountain trail, especially if riding it during the week. Realize that this trail is very popular with hikers and bikers and will be busy on the weekends. Shoes are a must and in winter ride with caution.

Notes:

MAP:

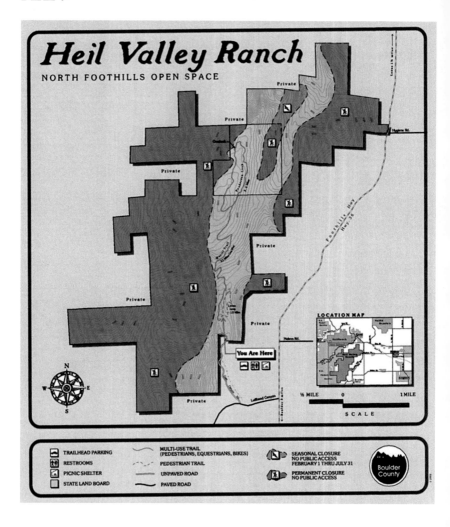

National Geographic #100

"The wind of heaven is that which blows between a horse's ears."
-Arabian Proverb

Trail #4
Trail Name:

Hall Ranch (Boulder)

Govt. Organization: Boulder County Open Space

Fees: None

Beginning Elevation: 5,499 ft.

Ending Elevation: 6,736 ft.

Trailer Parking: Parking easily accommodates 5 large trailers with ample room to maneuver. Pull in parking.

Facilities: At the trailhead, restrooms are available. Water is available for your horse from the river along the trail.

Difficulty: Difficult, bridge, rocky, steady climb and long trail

Length of Trail: Approximately 12 miles round trip riding using Nighthawk Trail and the Nelson Loop Trail.

Trail Usage: Horseback riding, hiking, biking
Dogs are not permitted.

Directions: Traveling I 25, turn west on Exit #243 (Ute Hwy/CO 66.) Travel approximately 7 miles to US 287. Cross this highway and continue. From the intersection of Ute Hwy/CO 66 and Hover Road in northern Longmont, continue heading west towards Lyons for 8 miles. Ute Hwy/CO 66 will dead end at a "T" intersection on the west side of Lyons. Turn south making a left onto CO 7 heading towards Allenspark. Drive along CO 7 out of Lyons for 1.2 miles. Look for trailhead parking on the north (right). The parking lot at Antelope Drive does NOT allow horse trailers.

Ample parking at trailhead

Restroom at trailhead

Picnic facilities at the trailhead

Nighthawk Trail takes off to the left (southwest)

Trail quickly becomes rocky

Small culvert to cross

Climb consists of many switchbacks

Trail passes through various open areas

Area becomes a little more wooded

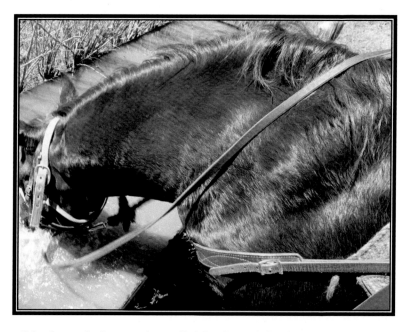

Much needed water is available about 3.5 miles into the trail

Stop and check out the stone wall along the trail

Perfect lunch stop with a beautiful view

At the top, the trail opens up into a large meadow

Trail is a 2.2 mile loop around the remains of the Hall Homestead

Bitterbrush Trail is an alternative route back to the trailhead

Crossing a bridge on the Nelson Loop Trail

Check out the remains of the Nelson Ranch

Completed the Nelson Loop Trail, return the way you came on Nighthawk Trail

General Information: If you and your horse are in shape and you have the time to ride a long trail, this is the place for you. Hall Ranch consists of 3,206 acres of backcountry. We rode the Nighthawk Trail (9.4 miles roundtrip, bikes are not allowed) and the Nelson Loop (2.2 miles). We could have returned on the Bitterbrush Trail (3.7 miles one way, hikers, bikers and equestrians) but we chose not to. I have been told that the Bitterbrush Trail is even rockier and more challenging than the Nighthawk Trail, so you decide.

The Nighthawk Trail overall is very rocky with just a few spots that are not. The trail is a very steady climb, "head-to-tail," with many switchbacks to facilitate the climb. Be sure to wear a hat and use sunscreen; there is very little shade for the first 3 miles. You may want to rest your horse along the way and take in the spectacular views that are available. Toward the end of the climb, stop at the watering tank to give your horse a drink and a rest. Along the way you may encounter groups of white-tailed deer. Near the top, various meadows give you the opportunity to stop for lunch or you might opt to wait and eat along the Nelson Loop Trail. We stopped at a meadow where we could view Longs Peak and Mount Meeker. Riding on, you find the Button Rock Trail, which branches off to the left (west) and is open to hikers only. A short distance from Button Rock Trail is the Nelson Loop Trail. We turned to the left (west) and rode the loop. Bikes are permitted here so be aware of what is behind and in front of you. You will encounter a small stream to cross as well as a wooden bridge. Along the loop the Bitterbrush Trail branches off descending to the trailhead. The Nelson Loop Trail is more wooded with openings to large meadows. If you have the time, stop and check out the Nelson Ranch. Finish the loop and connect with the Nighthawk Trail for your descent.

Hall Ranch is home to mountain lions and bobcats; bells on your horses would be wise. The prairie rattlesnake is also commonly seen here from March through October. These are highly used trails on the weekend, so plan to come early or ride during the week. Shoes are a must. If winter riding, call ahead to check the conditions.

Notes:

MAP:

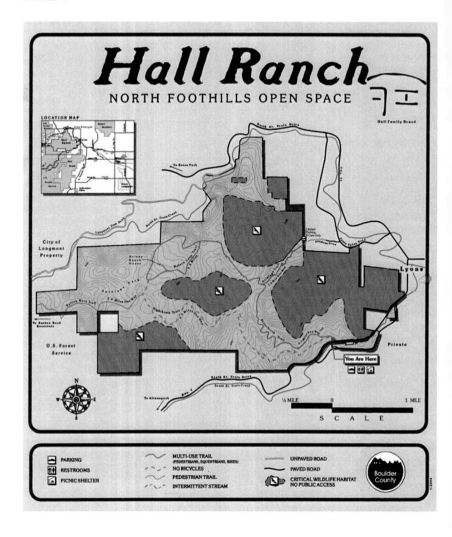

National Geographic #100

"There are times when you can trust a horse, times when you can't and times when you have to."
-Anonymous

Trail #5

Trail Name:

Lagerman Reservoir (Boulder)

Govt. Organization: Boulder County Parks & Open Space

Fees: None

Beginning Elevation: 5,065 ft.

Ending Elevation: 5,065 ft.

Trailer Parking: Parking easily accommodates large trailers with ample room to maneuver. There are no designated spots for horse trailers.

Facilities: At the trailhead, restrooms and domestic drinking water is available. Bring water for your horse.

Difficulty: Easy

Length of Trail: Approximately 1.6 miles round trip. There is a seasonal closure (April 1st through July 31st) on the western end of the reservoir for nesting birds.

Trail Usage: Horseback riding, hiking, biking
Dogs are permitted on a leash.

Directions: If approaching from the north on I 25, turn west on Exit #243 (Ute Hwy/CO 66). Travel approximately 7 miles to US 287. Cross this highway and continue past Hover Road. At the intersection of North 75th Street, turn south (left) and travel approximately 4.5 miles to Pike Road. Turn west (right) and travel for 1 mile turning south (left) into the entrance of the reservoir.

If approaching from the south on CO 119 South /Diagonal Hwy, head west (left) at Niwot Road for approximately ½ mile then north (right) on North 73rd Street. NOTE: North 73rd Street becomes North 75th Street. Travel approximately 3 miles. Turn west (left) on Pike Road then travel 1 mile. Turn south (left) into the entrance of Lagerman Reservoir.

Entrance

Ample Parking Area

Restroom Facilities

Trail allows "side-by-side" riding

Cement run-offs to ride over

Horse pastures borders part of the reservoir

Pump house

Picnic area at trailhead

General Information: So why would I want to ride my horse here? I see this location as a perfect ride for a young horse, a new rider, a newly purchased horse, a horse that has rarely been ridden outside of an arena or just a place to ride in the colder weather. There is a seasonal closure (April 1st through July 31st) on the western end of the reservoir for nesting birds. Bank and boat fishing are permitted and are restricted to wake-less speeds. Sailboats and sailboards are not allowed. The trail is dirt, so shoes are not required. The trail also allows you to ride "side-by-side" and has minimum distractions. There were horses in a northeast pasture, some prairie dog holes and cement run-offs as obstacles. Even though it is only a 1.6 mile loop, it can be ridden multiple times. Also, Pike Road, which runs along the north side of the reservoir, is dirt with minor traffic if you wanted to extend your ride.

Notes:

MAP:

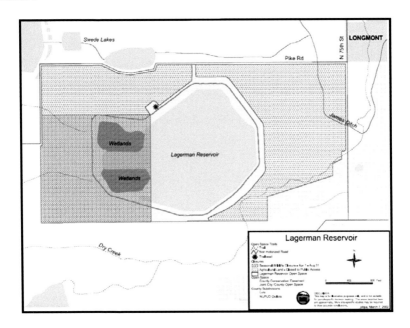

National Geographic #100

"Always smile when you are riding because it changes your intent."
–James Shaw

Trail #6
Trail Name:
Boulder Reservoir/Coot Lake (Boulder)

Govt. Organization: City of Boulder Parks & Recreation

Fees: Yes, if main parking lot at reservoir is used during the summer season. Call (303) 413-7200 for dates and fee information.

Beginning Elevation: 5,212 ft.

Ending Elevation: 5,212 ft.

Trailer Parking: Parking easily accommodates large trailers with ample room to maneuver in parking lot at main entrance on the west side. Parking is available at the Eagle lot further north. Small parking lot for 1 or 2 trailers further north where 51st becomes 55th.

Facilities: Restrooms at main entrance of reservoir and at Coot Lake

Difficulty: Easy

Length of Trail: Approximately 3.8 miles round trip loop (Boulder Reservoir Trail 2.6 miles, Coot Lake Trail 1.2)

Trail Usage: Horseback riding, hiking, biking (No bikes on Coot Lake Trail)
Dogs are permitted, unleashed if under "voice" command.

Directions: If approaching from the north on I 25, turn west on Exit #243 (Ute Hwy/CO 66). Travel approximately 7 miles to US 287. Cross this highway and continue past Hover Road. At the intersection of North 75th Street, turn south (left) and travel approximately 4.5 miles (75th Street becomes 73rd Street) to Niwot Road. Turn west (right) and travel approximately 2 miles to North 55th Street (this is an easy turn to miss). Turn south (left) on North 55th Street and travel for approximately 1 mile. The parking lot will be on the east (left). If parking is unavailable, continue for another mile to the Eagle lot on the west (right) on North 51st Street. The main entrance to Boulder Reservoir is further south on the east (left).

Small parking area at 51st/55th Street

Main entrance to Boulder Reservoir, park in lot on west side of gate

Eagle Trailhead parking lot on 51st Street

Crossing the outlet at the reservoir, notice the width of the bridge and the height of the "silo"

Trail is wide, allowing "side-by-side" riding

We continued right (west) around the reservoir

Trail follows 63rd Street, expect traffic noise

Riding across the dam

Trail officially ends here at the marina

Riding around the marina, toward the Main Entrance

One of the two turn offs to Coot Lake (southwest side of lake)

The other turn off to Coot Lake (southeast side of lake)

Bridge to cross along Coot Lake Trail

Trail around Coot Lake is wide allowing "side-by-side" riding

**Trail is fairly close to the lake at spots,
notice the traffic on 63rd Street**

**Need to ride through Coot Lake parking lot to get back
to Boulder Reservoir Trail**

General Information: This is another trail that I would ride only in the colder months when there is less usage of Boulder Reservoir. We rode it during a warmer day in December. The path is generally wide with small gravel where shoes are not needed. We rode both the Boulder Reservoir Trail as well as the Coot Lake Trail. We started at the parking lot near 55th and 51st. The first obstacle that we met was the very narrow bridge that went over a ditch. A wide horse with saddlebags will rub up against the railings. Notice the cap of the "silo." This cap was just about eye level for my horse. We dismounted and walked our horses across this bridge. From here it was just ride and enjoy the views.

The Coot Lake Trail has two entry points from the Boulder Reservoir Trail. I would suggest riding around Coot Lake prior to crossing the dam on Boulder Reservoir. The Coot Lake Trail is very relaxing with various informational signs posted along the way. At some point, you will need to ride through the Coot Lake parking area as well as across a minor bridge. After finishing Coot Lake Trail, you will be back on the Boulder Reservoir Trail. Expect to hear traffic noises as well as a possible train in the distance as you cross the reservoir.

At the south end of the reservoir, the trail officially ends. From here you can turn around and return or ride around the outskirts of the marina parking lot toward the main entrance of the park on 51st Street. Be aware that there are many "scary" canvas covered boats along the way. After reaching the Main Entrance, continue right (north) on 51st Street for approximately 1 ¼ miles back to the parking lot and your horse trailer. 51st Street starts out paved but quickly becomes dirt. You will pass the Eagle Nest parking lot on your left (west). In another ½ mile or so, you will pass a parking lot on the right (east) side of the road that is used by individuals that fly model airplanes. Be aware that even though this is a dirt road, the traffic can be moderately heavy at times and drivers are not expecting to see horses on the road. If you ride this trail when the reservoir is open for swimming and boating, expect all types of distractions for your horse.

Notes:

MAP:

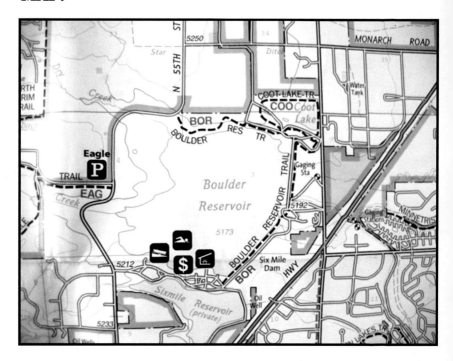

National Geographic #100

"A good trainer can hear a horse speak to him. A great trainer can hear him whisper."
–Monty Roberts

Trail #7

Trail Name:

Boulder Valley Ranch (Boulder)

Govt. Organization: City of Boulder Open Space & Mountain Parks

Fees: None

Beginning Elevation: 5,242 ft.

Ending Elevation: 5,575 ft.

Trailer Parking: Ranch parking lot - 15-20 trailers
Eagle parking lot - 8 trailers
There is ample room for maneuvering, please park with consideration for cars as well as other horse trailers.

Facilities: Restrooms at Longhorn Road west parking lot (car parking only)

Difficulty: Easy to Easy-Moderate

Length of Trail: Numerous loops of approximately 2-3 miles each

Trail Usage: Horseback riding, hiking, biking, no bikes are permitted on the Cobalt Trail and Mesa Reservoir Trail.
Dogs are permitted and can be off leash if under voice and sight control.

Directions: If approaching from the north on I 25, turn west on Exit #243 (Ute Hwy/CO 66). Travel approximately 7 miles to US 287. Cross this highway and continue past Hover Road. At the intersection of North 75th Street, turn south (left) and travel approximately 4.5 miles to Niwot Road. Turn west (right) and travel approximately 2 miles to North 55th Street (this is an easy turn to miss.) Turn south (left) on North 55th Street and travel for approximately 2 miles. The Eagle lot will be on the west (right). To reach the Boulder Valley Ranch parking lot if approaching from the north, take US 36 south. At Longhorn Road turn east (left) and travel for 1 ½ miles on the dirt road to the ranch. Turn left into the ranch and park at the far northeast open area.

**Entry to parking at Ranch area (I was leaving the area)
Do NOT park in the lot on the right (west)**

Horse trailer parking at the Ranch

Cobalt Trail starting from the Ranch parking area

Prairie Dog holes are plentiful on the Ranch

Rocky spot on Cobalt Trail

Most of Cobalt Trail is "side-by-side" riding

Expect to hear and see "scary" things on the Cobalt Trail

Remember to leave gates as you found them

Trails are well marked

Gates are abundant throughout the Ranch

Steps will be encountered at various spots along the trails

Watch the footing around the culverts

Riding along the dam

Most times, water is available for your horse at a small pond

Expect to hear gun fire as you pass a shooting range located in the distance

Sections of the trail can be rocky and a little steep

General Information: Boulder Valley Ranch is presently a working and historic ranch. While riding on the Cobalt Trail, you can see the remnants of a smelter on the south side of Longhorn Road. The trails are in the open with very few trees so be sure to have a hat, sunscreen and water for yourself. Prairie dogs as well as rattlesnakes are abundant on the Ranch. Watch your step and keep on the trail as much as possible. The Ranch consists of various trails that allow you to choose distance and difficulty. When riding here, I usually park at the Ranch parking area (15-20 trailer spaces) off of Longhorn Road. Longhorn Road starts out paved but quickly becomes dirt. Be aware that the road can be extremely rutted and needs to be traveled at a very slow speed. About 75% of the trails can be ridden "side-by-side." A very easy ride is to park at the Eagle parking lot off of 51st Street and ride the Eagle/Sage loop (see map) on the east side of the Ranch. This loop may be done without shoes and offers few distractions and minimum gates. The Left Hand Trail I will cover as a separate trail (Trail #8).

The remaining trails (Cobalt, Mesa Reservoir, Hidden Valley, Deggee, Old Mill and the western portion of Eagle) have numerous gates, rocky areas, slight climbs and descents as well as noise and sight distractions (coffee store, maintenance shops & shooting range).

I would suggest shoes on your horses as well as knowing your horse's limitations. I would rate this area easy to moderate. I have ridden this area year round, but would suggest spring and fall. Summer could be very hot with the little shade available. Winter riding is possible, but I would suggest checking out the site first. This is a heavily used area. If riding on the weekend, get there early. Rattlesnakes are prevalent during the late spring and summer months.

Notes:

MAP:

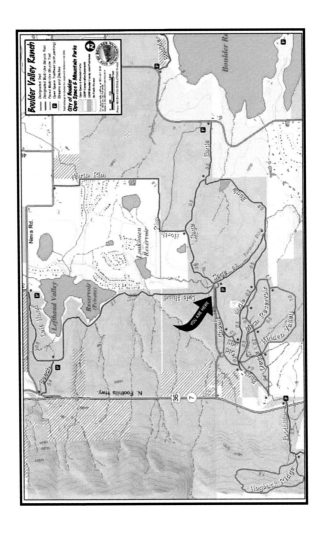

National Geographic #100
Or
City of Boulder Official Open Space & Mountain Parks Trails map
2002   (303-441-3440)

"A man on a horse is spiritually as well as physically bigger than a man on foot."
–John Steinbeck

Trail #8
Trail Name:
Left Hand Trail At Boulder Valley Ranch (Boulder)

Govt. Organization: City of Boulder Open Space & Mountain Parks

Fees: None

Beginning Elevation: 5,242 ft.

Ending Elevation: 5,575 ft.

Trailer Parking: Eagle parking lot - 8 trailers
Left Hand parking lot - 8 trailers
Ranch parking lot - 15-20 trailers
There is ample room for maneuvering, please park with consideration for cars as well as other horse trailers.
The Beech parking lot & Picnic Pavilion is rented out by the Boulder County Open Space for large groups of 25 riders or more for a small fee. Do NOT park at the Beech parking lot if you are not part of a large group that has rented the area for the day.

Facilities: Restrooms at Longhorn Road west parking lot (car parking only). Restrooms are also located at Beech Picnic area.

Difficulty: Easy with various bridges to cross and small hills.

Length of Trail: If parking at the Eagle parking lot and riding to the Left Hand parking lot, the ride is approximately 9.5 miles roundtrip. From the Ranch parking lot to the Left Hand parking lot, the ride is approximately 6 miles roundtrip.

Trail Usage: Horseback riding, hiking, biking
Dogs must be on a hand-held leash on the designated trail and are prohibited off trail.

Directions: See Boulder Valley Ranch (Trail #7) for directions

Parking at the Eagle lot off of 51ˢᵗ Street

Riding along the Eagle Trail where it branches to the Sage Trail

A small bridge to cross. Horses may be grazing in this pasture

The gate you want is to your right (north east).
At this point, you have gone too far!!

Finally, you are on the Left Hand Trail

Trail crosses a road into a development

Long wooden bridge to cross (no water)

Another small wooden bridge (no water)

We counted "7" gates on the Left Hand Trail

Restroom at the Beech Picnic area

Beech Picnic Pavilion located along the Left Hand Trail

Parking lot for renters of the Beech Picnic Pavilion

Another bridge to cross as you approach the Left Hand Trail parking lot

Left Hand Trail parking lot at Neva Road & 39th Street

Other horseback riders on the trail

Left Hand Trail ends at Neva Road

General Information: Dubbed the Left Hand Trail after Chief Niwot (which means left hand in Arapaho), the relatively flat trail stretches from the intersection of Neva Road and 39th Street south for three miles one way to connect with a vast trail network at Boulder Valley Ranch. When we rode this trail, we parked at the Eagle lot, adding 1 ½ miles one way. We started the ride on the Eagle Trail. At the "Y" where Eagle and Sage trails meet, we took the right (north) fork (Sage Trail) and continued to ride toward the Ranch. Passing the Ranch on your left (south) continue over a small bridge and through a pasture where horses may be grazing. A short distance from the bridge will be a gate and another parking lot across the road. Do NOT go through the gate but look to your right (north/east) for another gate. There are no signs stating that this is the Left Hand Trail. Ride through the first of the 7 gates on this trail, then up and down a small hill. Be aware that this is a blind spot for travelers coming in the opposite direction. Be sure to leave all of the gates as you found them. The remaining trail is relatively flat, no trees and a few small hills to climb gradually. At one point you cross a paved road and will pass the Lake Valley neighborhood. As you continue on the trail, over a few bridges and past prairie dog conservation areas, the Beech Pavilion and restroom will come into view. You can see the Lefthand Valley Reservoir, a private reservoir along your ride. The trail passes through a field of mixed grasses to the Lefthand parking lot. Continuing past the parking lot, the trail ends at Neva Road. If you wish, you can travel east along Neva Road approximately 1 mile and pick up the North Rim Trail and head south connecting to the Sage Trail. We chose not to do this and returned the way we came.

This is a very nice ride and would be good for a beginner horse that has some experience. In the summer, expect it to be hot with the likelihood of encountering rattlesnakes. Shoes are not needed and you can ride this trail year round. The trail allows some "side-by-side" riding, but the majority is "head-to-tail."

Notes:

Map:

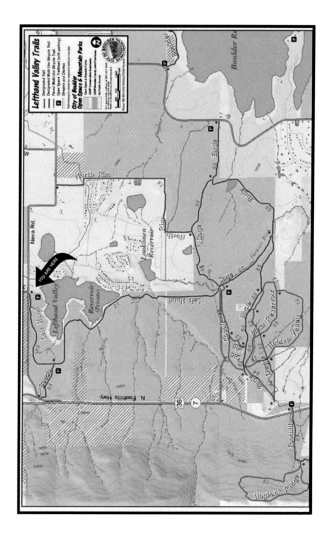

National Geographic #100
Or
City of Boulder Official Open Space & Mountain Parks Trails map
2002   (303-441-3440)

"A horse gallops with his lungs, perseveres with his heart and wins with his character."
–Frederico Tesio

Trail #9

Trail Name:

Teller Farm (Boulder)

Govt. Organization: City of Boulder Open Space & Mountain Parks

Fees: None

Beginning Elevation: 5,200 ft.

Ending Elevation: 5,200 ft.

Trailer Parking: Teller Farm North - South side of Valmont Road between 75th and 95th Streets
Teller Farm South – North side of Arapahoe Road between 75th and 95th Streets.
Both lots easily accommodate large trailers. Each lot could park 6-8 trailers depending on size and the number of other cars. Teller Farm South parking lot seems to be less used.

Facilities: Restroom facilities at Teller Farm South parking lot only.

Difficulty: Easy

Length of Trail: Approximately 6.6 miles round trip

Trail Usage: Horseback riding, hiking, biking
Dogs are permitted and can be off leash if under voice and sight control.

Directions: From I 25, take CO 52 (Exit 235). Drive west to 95th Street (8.0 miles). Turn south (left) on 95th Street and continue south to Valmont Road (2.0 miles). Turn west (right) on Valmont Road and travel 0.5 miles. The Teller Farm North parking lot is on the left.

To park at the Teller Farm South parking lot, continue traveling south on 95th street, past Valmont Road to Arapahoe Road (2.0 miles). Turn west (right) on Arapahoe Road and travel approximately 1.75 miles. The Teller Farm South parking lot is on your right.

Parking lot at Teller Farm North

Parking lot at Teller Farm South

Two or three gates to open along the Teller Farm Trail

One of the bridges to cross

Llamas may be a challenge to your horse

Trail winds through a working cattle ranch

A different type of bridge to cross

Another obstacle for your horse to encounter

Trail is wide allowing "side-by-side" riding and if you feel comfortable with it, a trot or canter

Irrigation equipment along side the trail

General Information: Teller Farm is named for Henry Teller, who founded the Colorado Central Railroad, was one of Colorado's two first senators and served as the Secretary of the Interior for President Chester A. Arthur. As you ride the trail you will meander through farmland used for crop production, cattle and horse grazing, and bee keeping. You will also pass Teller Lake, a wildlife preserve.

Teller Farm Trail is dirt and gravel that is flat and wide enough to ride "side-by-side." Shoes are not needed. Obstacles include a couple of wooden bridges along the way that are wide and well made. If your horse has never crossed a bridge, this is a good "first" bridge. At the time we rode, on the east side of the trail was the home of a few llamas. This could become an "exciting" introduction of a new animal for your horse. Being a working ranch, expect to ride through grazing cattle as well. Along the east side of the trail is an irrigation ditch along with the irrigation equipment. Toward Teller Farm North trailhead is a large oil tank. Also at this end are the stockyard and buildings, and you may encounter moving farm equipment.

This is a trail that one can ride year round, weather permitting. It's a good "first" ride in the spring, first trail ride on a new horse or first trail ride for a beginner rider. There seemed to be plenty of room to maneuver off the trail if needed.

We parked in the Teller Farm North parking lot. Like most trailheads, the earlier you get there, the better chance of a good parking space. From this parking lot you can also ride the White Rocks Trail (Trail #10) and the East Boulder/Gunbarrel Farm Trail (Trail #11).

Notes:

MAP:

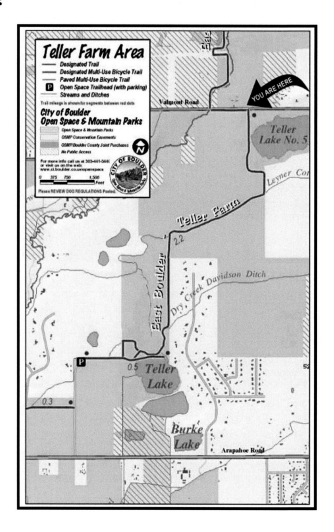

National Geographic #100
Or
City of Boulder Official Open Space & Mountain Parks Trails map
2002   (303-441-3440)

"There is something about the outside of a horse that is good for the inside of a man."
–Sir Winston Churchill

Trail #10
Trail Name:

White Rocks Trail (Boulder)

Govt. Organization: City of Boulder Open Space & Mountain Parks

Fees: None

Beginning Elevation: 5,200 ft.

Ending Elevation: 5,400 ft.

Trailer Parking: Teller Farm North - South side of Valmont Road between 75th and 95th Streets (Parking easily accommodates large trailers with ample room to maneuver.)
White Rocks Trailhead – A very small parking lot (approx. 10 cars) on 95th Street just north of W. Phillips Road

Facilities: Restrooms are not available at either trailhead

Difficulty: Easy

Length of Trail: 5.6 miles round trip from Teller Farm North to White Rocks Trailhead on 95th Street

Trail Usage: Horseback riding, hiking, biking
Dogs are Not permitted.

Directions: From I 25, take CO 52 (Exit 235). Drive west to 95th Street (8.0 miles). Turn south (left) on 95th Street and continue south to Valmont Road (2.0 miles). Turn west (right) on Valmont Road and travel 0.5 miles. The Teller Farm North parking lot is on the left.

Teller Farm North parking lot

Small parking lot west of 95ᵗʰ Street at W. Phillips Road

Entrance to White Rocks Trailhead from Teller Farm North

Trail crosses Valmont Road from the Teller Farm North trailhead

Beginning of the White Rocks Trailhead from Valmont Road

Ride beside Dry Creek (which isn't!!)

Trail is well marked and easy to follow

Cross an abandoned railroad track

Trail is wide enough to ride "side-by-side" 50% of the way

Crossing Boulder Creek

Crossing another bridge before a small climb

Stay on the trail

Massive homes attract your attention along the trail

Cross private road to stay on the White Rocks Trail

At "Y" turn right (east) toward White Rocks Trailhead at
95th Street and W. Phillips Road

Last stretch along a housing development before end of trail

General Information: We rode this starting at the Teller Farm North trailhead. The trail starts at an opening at the northwest corner of the parking lot and travels about 200 yards following Valmont Road. Here you need to cross the road to pick up the main trail. Note that this is a fairly busy street so be careful. The trail starts out crossing private land, with the owner allowing access. The trail passes by an award-winning pond. Flatirons Gravel won the award (from the Wildlife Society and the National Sand & Gravel Assn.) for their reclamation efforts here. As you cross the bridge at Boulder Creek, you can see the White Rock Cliffs to the west. Be aware that there may be water fowl under or near the bridge.

From here the trail rises steeply across the ridge, then turns to climb more slowly and steadily. The scenery includes the foothills as well as some massive homes. The trail tops off, then further on drops and climbs again. You finally crest out, ride down a short decline and then cross a private drive. After a short distance you come to a "Y." Take the right (east) fork and continue on the White Rocks Trail for another .5 miles to the trailhead at 95th Street and W. Phillips Road. If you take the left (west) fork at the "Y," you will be on the East Boulder/Gunbarrel Farm Trail (see Trail #11).

I would see this as a trail for a horse and rider with some experience on trails because of the road and bridge crossings, the small increase in elevation, and the close proximity to a housing subdivision. The terrain is fairly open and would be hot during the summer. Also, due to the water (ponds and streams), expect mosquitoes. Hat, sunscreen and mosquito spray may be necessary. Shoes are not needed on this trail and it can be ridden year round (check first for conditions). Approximately 50 % of the trail can be ridden "side-by-side." This trail can be combined with the Teller Farm Trail (Trail # 9) and the East Boulder/Gunbarrel Farm Trail (Trail #11) for a longer ride.

Notes:

MAP:

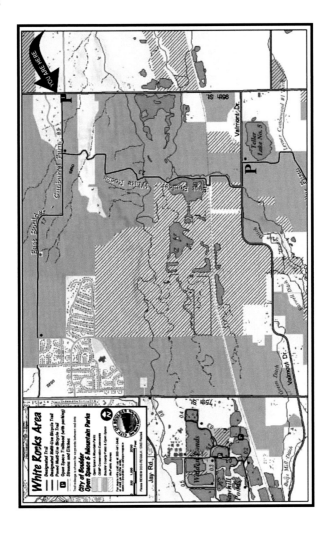

National Geographic #100
Or
City of Boulder Official Open Space & Mountain Parks Trails map
2002   (303-441-3440)

"And God took a handful of southerly wind, blew His breath over it and created the horse."
–Bedouin Legend

Trail #11
Trail Name:
East Boulder/Gunbarrel Farm (Boulder)

Govt. Organization: City of Boulder Open Space & Mountain Parks

Fees: None

Beginning Elevation: 5,123 ft.

Ending Elevation: 5,394 ft.

Trailer Parking: White Rocks Trailhead – A very small parking lot (approx. 10 cars) on 95th Street, just north of W. Phillips Road

Facilities: None

Difficulty: Easy

Length of Trail: Approximately 4.40 miles round trip

Trail Usage: Horseback riding, hiking, biking
Dogs are Not permitted on the .5 mile of the White Rocks Trail.
Dogs are permitted and can be off leash if under voice and sight control on the East Boulder/Gunbarrel Farm portion of the trail.

Directions: From I 25, take CO 52 (Exit 235). Drive west to 95th Street (8.0 miles). Turn south (left) on 95th Street. The parking lot is on the west (right), just north of W. Phillips Road.

Small parking lot west of 95th Street at W. Phillips Road

Starts as White Rocks Trail and passes a housing development

Continue straight (west) on the Gunbarrel Farm Trail

Trail slowly climbs toward a water tank in the distance

Continue on the trail to the right (north)

Trail maintains a slow climb

The water tower is the climax of your climb

Stay on the trail to avoid the low guide wires at the water tower

You may ride your horse off the trail

Horses in the Open Space Area

116

General Information: We started the trail at the small parking lot off 95th Street. If you were to ride on a weekend, you might have trouble parking here (See Trail #10 for an alternative.) The first .5 mile of this trail is part of the White Rocks Trail. Dogs are not allowed on this section. The trail is wide and follows the back property lines of a housing development. At the .5 mile mark you could travel left (south) and continue on the White Rocks Trail. We chose to continue straight on the East Boulder/Gunbarrel Farm trail. Dogs are now permitted on the trail, without a leash, if under voice and sight control. The trail is fairly wide and allows for riding "side-by-side," conditions permitting. It is a steady climb to the top at the site of a water tower. Along the way you will notice signs designating this as an Open Space Area with Lookout Road as the northern border. You may ride here but be aware that it is fenced in some spots with very few exit gates so you may have to backtrack to get out. At the water tower there are low guide/tension wires, so stay in the middle of the trail or off to the south side. Continue straight and down the hill toward the trailhead at Boulderado Dr & Cambridge St in the Heatherwood neighborhood.

This is a pleasant, easy ride for a beginning horse or rider. The only obstacles would be the bikes and dogs. This trail is dirt and can be ridden without shoes and year round (check conditions). There is a small climb but it is gradual and the trail is fairly short. It is heavily used, especially on the weekends, so arrive early for a parking space on 95th.

Notes:

MAP:

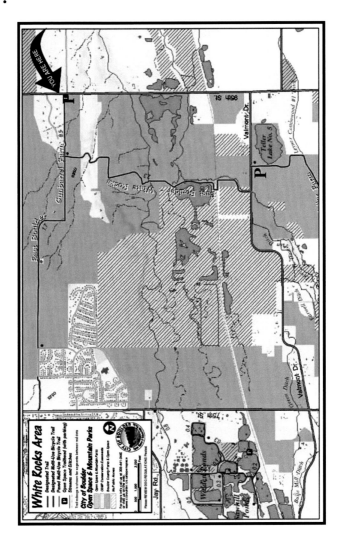

National Geographic #100
Or
City of Boulder Official Open Space & Mountain Parks Trails map
2002   (303-441-3440)

"Riding: The art of keeping a horse between you and the ground."
-Anonymous

Trail #12
Trail Name:

Walden–Sawhill Ponds (Boulder)

Govt. Organization: City of Boulder Open Spaces & Mountain Parks

Fees: None

Beginning Elevation: 5,125 ft.
Ending Elevation: 5,125 ft.

Trailer Parking: Ample parking for 2-3 trailers at 1st parking lot. Larger parking lot further down road but may have distractions with equipment/trucks at the gravel pit. No designated spots for horse trailers.

Facilities: At the various trailheads, restrooms are available. Picnic tables, grills and a group shelter are available on a "first come" basis.

Difficulty: Easy

Length of Trail: 4 miles round trip via various loops

Trail Usage: Horseback riding, hiking, biking, fishing
Dogs are permitted on a leash.

Directions: Approaching from the north, take CO 119/Diagonal Hwy south to Jay Road. Turn east (left) on Jay Road and continue traveling for approximately 2 ½ miles. At North 75th Street turn south (right) and continue for approximately 1 mile. A sign to "Walden/Sawmill Ponds" will be on the west (right) side of the road.

1st parking area at Walden Ponds off of 75th Street

2nd parking area at Walden Ponds, notice the active gravel pit

Parking area at Sawhill Ponds

Picnic area and restrooms at 1st parking area at Walden Ponds

Expect to have water fowl crossing your path or flying overhead

Large trucks travel on the road to your left from this gravel pit

**Trails loop among the various ponds,
travel is mostly "head-to-tail"**

Railroad tracks line the south side of the Sawhill Ponds

Trails are not well marked but the paths are easy to follow among the various ponds

Some areas can be a little "marshy"

Some portions of the trail are wide enough to ride "side-by-side"

Keep an eye out for obstacles that could be dangerous

Expect to see beautiful views of the mountains as well as an abundant variety of birds and small animals

The ponds are still in the process of being "reclaimed"

General Information: The Walden–Sawhill Ponds are gravel pits that are being reclaimed from the blemished landscape, creating a wildlife habitat and a series of trails around the ponds for everyone to enjoy. We parked at the 1st parking lot on the right (north) as you enter from 75th Street. From here the trail follows the road on your left (south) to the main parking lot for Walden Ponds with ponds on your right (north). As you travel this portion of the trail expect to see gravel trucks on the road going to and from the active gravel pit. Follow the trail past the main parking lot and the active gravel pit. Expect to hear noise and see movement that might make your horse a little apprehensive. If choosing to park at the main parking lot, be sure to take the noise and machinery into consideration. The trails around the ponds are dirt and shoes are not necessary. The majority of the trail is "head-to-tail" with about 20% of the trail allowing you to ride "side-by-side."

The best way to describe how to ride this trail is to say that you and your horse will meander among the various ponds. Seeing that this reclamation is a work-in-progress, be aware that there are some hazards yet to be cleaned up and you need to watch where you ride. Expect to see all types of water fowl. Don't be surprised to be buzzed by landing geese as you ride the trail. Raptors are also prevalent. This is a very relaxing ride once you get beyond the gravel pit. As of this writing, the railroad tracks are not active. This is another trail that can be ridden year round. I suggest that you check the conditions prior to riding during the winter months. Riding on the weekend may also eliminate the noise and moving trucks from the gravel pit.

Notes:

MAP:

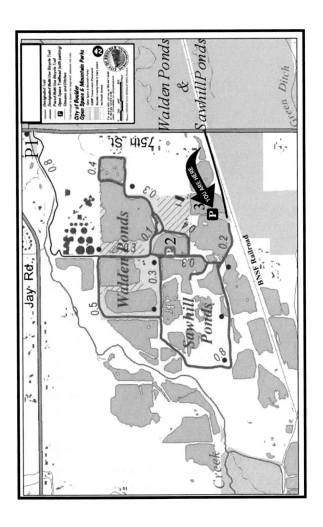

National Geographic #100
Or
City of Boulder Official Open Space & Mountain Parks Trails map
2002   (303-441-3440)

"Is it the smell of their body as I hug their long neck, or the scent only a horse has that I can't forget? Is it the depth of their eyes as they contentedly rest? No, it's just being around them that I like the best."
–Teresa Becker

128

Trail #13
Trail Name:

Niwot Trail (Boulder)

Govt. Organization: City of Boulder Open Space & Mountain Parks

Fees: None

Beginning Elevation: 5,108 ft.

Ending Elevation: 5,201 ft.

Trailer Parking: If parking off Monarch Road, the parking easily accommodates large trailers with ample room to maneuver. Parking at the 79th Street lot is not recommended due to the small lot and the recycling bins. There are no designated spots for trailers at either parking lot.

Facilities: No restrooms or water at either parking lot.

Difficulty: Easy to Moderate (bridges to cross, 79th Street to cross)

Length of Trail: Approximately 5.5 miles round trip from the Monarch parking lot and taking the right (east) fork at the third bridge. Add approximately 2 miles if you also ride the trail after taking the left (west) fork at the third bridge.

Trail Usage: Horseback riding, hiking, biking
Dogs are permitted on a leash.

Directions: Heading west on Ute Hwy/CO 66 turn south (left) onto Hover Road and travel for 4.2 miles. Make a slight right onto CO 119 South /Diagonal Hwy and travel for approximately 4.7 miles. Turn east (left) onto Monarch Road for approximately 1 mile. The parking lot will be on your right.

Parking Area at Monarch Road

Very limited parking at 79th Street, not recommended

First gate encountered southwest of the Monarch Road parking lot

Notice the plastic at the bottom of this gate

First of the various bridges that you have to cross

Prairie dog holes line the trail

Pass through gate, cross road to the parking lot on 79th Street

Bridge on the north side of the 79th Street parking lot

Trail is fine gravel and wide enough to ride "side-by-side"

Trail splits; we took the trail to the right

Trail passes through fields skirting a housing development

Crossing a road in the housing development

Obey signs and do not ride in the Somerset's private pathways

Other riders we met on the trail

General Information: This is another great trail that can be ridden, weather permitting, year round. Located just south of the small town of Niwot, the trail can be accessed from two parking lots. I would suggest parking at the Monarch Road parking lot. The 79th Street parking lot is extremely small and contains the recycling bins as well. I will describe the trail from Monarch Road.

The entrance to the trail is in the southeast corner of the parking lot. The gates are spring loaded and we found it easier just to dismount and open/close the gates. Also, it is best to stay on the trail as much as possible due to the numerous prairie dog holes along both sides of the trail. On this portion of the trail, a gate and fences have the lower half covered in plastic. On a windy day this may be a problem with your horse. The first bridge that you cross is padded with rubber, giving it a different sound and feel. You will travel approximately .8 mile before you reach a gate and cross 79th Street. This road can be very busy so I would suggest that you dismount and walk across. Also, in the 79th Street parking lot are the recycling bins. Be aware that people may be putting cans in these bins and may not hear or see you and your horse. This could be potentially a scary item for your horse. When you cross the bridge just north of this parking lot, plastic bags (for dog duty) hang near the far end of the bridge. Again, this may be something that may frighten your horse. At the next bridge crossing, you will come to a "Y" in the trail. If you take the left (west) fork, this trail will go for approximately 1 mile before you will have to turn around. You will encounter additional bridges and more of a "city" atmosphere here. We took the right (east) fork and proceeded along the trail that skirts the houses, past various small ponds. Eventually, you will cross a road that is an entrance road to the development. Also, the housing community is still growing so expect to hear construction type noises as well as barking dogs that may come running up to their fence edge. No shoes are needed on this trail and you can ride "side-by-side." I rated this easy to moderate because of the bridges and the various "city" type noises that could be challenging to a "green" horse or rider.

Notes:

MAP:

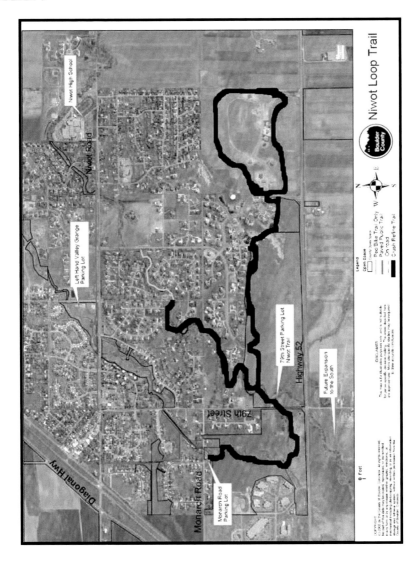

National Geographic #100

"Gypsy gold does not chink and glitter. It gleams in the sun and neighs in the dark."
–Gypsy Saying

Trail #14
Trail Name:

Barr Lake State Park (Adams)

Govt. Organization: Colorado State Parks (303) 659-6005

Fees: Yes, at time of this writing $5.00/day

Beginning Elevation: 5,100 ft.

Ending Elevation: 5,100 ft.

Trailer Parking: Ample parking for 15-20 trailers

Facilities: Restrooms with water for you and your horse

Difficulty: Easy to moderate (approximately 1 mile of riding near active railroad tracks)

Length of Trail: 8.8 miles roundtrip

Trail Usage: Horseback riding, hiking, biking, boating
Dogs are permitted on a leash.

Directions: From I 25 take Exit #229 east towards Brighton for 9.0 miles. Turn on US 85 south (right) for approximately 1 mile. Turn east (left) on Bromley Lane and travel for 4.2 miles. This road turns into E 152nd Ave for .8 mile. Turn south (right) on Picadilly Road and travel for 2.2 miles. The entrance to the park will be on the west (right) side of the road.

Park fee deposited here, if not collected at Ranger Station

Parking is near Nature Center (currently being improved)

First bridge out of the parking lot has a high "crest" and some horses may refuse to walk over it

Alternate bridge a short distance to the east by the boat ramp

Trail surrounds the lake, is well marked and allows "side-by-side" riding

A smaller bridge you must cross

Sheep in the pasture

Next 1 ¼ miles you ride beside active railroad tracks

Trail is extremely close to the tracks for the 1st ¼ mile

Trail allows you to get a little further away from the RR tracks into a small field

Hunting blinds east of the dam

Beautiful views of the mountains

General Information: Barr Lake is an 815 acre park situated just outside of Brighton. The trail is flat, comprised of both, dirt and a dirt and pea gravel mix that surrounds a lake for 8.8 miles. This is a trail that could be ridden year round, depending on the weather. Be sure to call ahead for trail conditions. From October 1st through the end of February, hunters are permitted to hunt on the east side of the dam on Wednesday and Saturday. I was assured that the blinds were far enough away that the hunting would not be dangerous to a horse on the trail. Personally, I would avoid riding Wednesdays and Saturdays during this time. At the beginning of the trail is an arched wooden bridge that could present a slight problem. When your horse attempts to cross it, the other side is hidden because of the high "crest," therefore frightening the horse. If your horse will not cross, ride to the northeast to the boat launching area and cross the bridge there. Another situation that you will have to consider is the active railroad that runs trains from 4 to 5 times daily on the northwest side of the park. The tracks run along the path for a little over a mile and are situated so that you can see and hear a train from a great distance away. The first ¼ mile is extremely close to the tracks with no place to escape if a train is going by. The remaining portion of the trail is routed into a small field that runs beside and further away from the train tracks. I would suggest that if you decide to ride this stretch, check to see if you see or can hear a train before you start this portion and gallop or trot as fast as you can through this section. You can also decide not to continue and turn around for a total ride of about 6 miles. If you stay on the loop, the next possible obstacle you may need to consider is the hunters in the blinds. Of course, if you don't ride during hunting season on Wednesday or Saturday, this won't be an issue. For our ride, we were able to miss the trains and the hunters, resulting in a very pleasurable ride. I would consider this trail "easy" if your horse crosses bridges easily and you miss the trains and hunters. Otherwise, I would consider this to be a "moderate" trail and not for a green horse or rider. I believe the views would be different for each season and very beautiful no matter what time of the year you rode the trail. Insect spray in the summer would be a must for you and your horse.

Notes:

MAP:

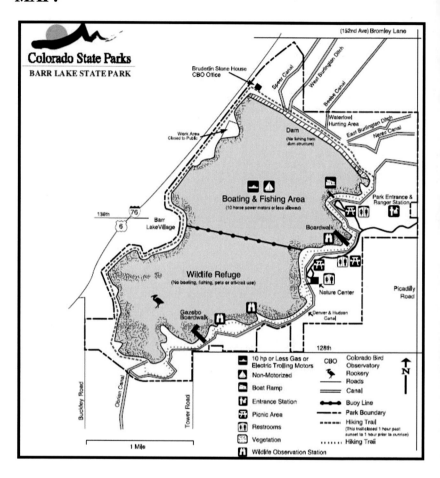

"Don't give your son money. As far as you can afford it, give him horses."
–Winston Churchill

Trail #15
Trail Name:

Mesa Trail (Boulder)

Govt. Organization: City of Boulder Open Space & Mountain Parks

Fees: No

Beginning Elevation: 5,638 ft.

Ending Elevation: 6,445 ft.

Trailer Parking: Room for two trailers at Mesa Trailhead
Room for eight trailers at Doudy Draw parking lot
on the south side of CO 170/Eldorado Springs Drive

Facilities: Restrooms at Mesa Trailhead as well as picnic tables. Bring water for yourself and your horse

Difficulty: Easy (1st 2 miles) to Moderate

Length of Trail: 16 miles round trip

Trail Usage: Horseback riding, hiking
Dogs are permitted on a leash.

Directions: Travel west on CO 128 to CO 93. Turn north (right) on CO 93 and travel 1.2 miles to CO 170/Eldorado Springs Drive. There will be a stop light and a small convenience store at the intersection. Turn west (left) and continue for approximately 1.5 miles to parking lots. I recommend that you use the Doudy Draw parking lot on the south (left) side and walk your horse across the street to the north Mesa Trail Trailhead. The Mesa Trail parking area itself can become very crowded and it's easy to get blocked in at this lot.

Parking at Doudy Draw parking lot

**Park along the left (south) side of circle next to the fence
at the Mesa Trailhead**

Entrance to trailhead

Small concrete bridge to cross over running water

Bridge to cross shortly after starting the trail

Trail starts out as gravel and allows "side-by-side" riding

Trail is well marked

Trail will become narrow and rocky. Steps can be found in various spots on the trail.

Trail winds through various meadows

Trail is steep, narrow, rocky and heavily wooded in places

Sections of the trail can be extremely rocky

Stop and let your horse drink at this small stream

A group of winding steps

These steps were narrow and had irregular spacing

Another set of steps

We took the left fork here and rode to a dead end

Just one of the spectacular views along the trail

The Dunn House located near the beginning of the trailhead

General Information: We rode this trail in the middle of the week and the trailhead was rather crowded. This is a very popular hiking trail and I'm sure that the weekend would be extremely busy. We parked at Doudy Draw on the south side of Eldorado Springs Drive and walked our horses across the street to the Mesa Trail Trailhead. Mountain lions and bears are common on the trail so I suggest that you have bells on your horse.

We started out by going over two different types of bridges with running water passing under the bridges. The first few miles of the trail, we climbed slowly on a gravel/dirt trail and were able to ride "side-by-side." As we climbed higher, the trail became rockier and narrower with lots of close-in foliage. The remaining portion of the trail is mostly "head-to-tail" riding.

Be sure your horse can handle steps on a trail. I felt that we encountered more steps than we normally found on a trail. Some of the steps were placed closer together than what we were normally accustomed to. It also seemed that many of the steps were located in steep sections of the trail.

The trail winds through various meadows as well as heavily wooded areas. The views along the way are spectacular: the Flatirons as well as Boulder to the northeast. The mountain meadows had plenty of green grass for a quick snack for our horses. We found the trail to be fairly well marked even though we did take a wrong turn riding to a dead end. Unfortunately, we had to cut our ride short to 8.5 miles roundtrip due to a storm approaching the area. I'm sure we will be back to ride the trail to the end.

The first part of the trail is easy but once the trail narrows, I would rate it as moderate. I wouldn't consider this a trail for a green horse or beginner rider. If you have the time, check out the historic Dunn House near the trailhead. This would be an awesome ride in the fall!!

Notes:

MAP:

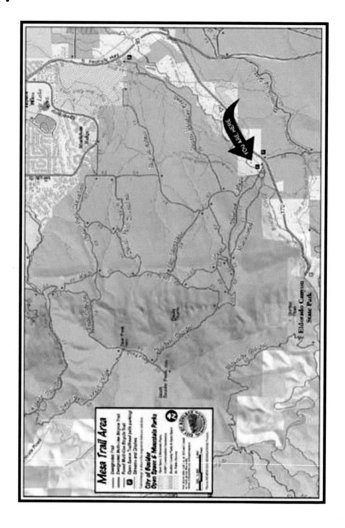

National Geographic #100
Or
City of Boulder Official Open Space & Mountain Parks Trails map
2002   (303-441-3440)

"Riding a horse is not a gentle hobby, to be picked up and laid down like a game of solitaire. It is a grand passion."
-Emerson

Trail #16
Trail Name:

Doudy Draw/Flatirons Vista (Boulder)

Govt. Organization: City of Boulder Open Space & Mountain Parks

Fees: None

Beginning Elevation: 5,638 ft.

Ending Elevation: 6,140 ft.

Trailer Parking: Ample room at both the Doudy Draw and Flatirons Vista parking lots for 6-8 trailers

Facilities: Restroom and picnic table available at about .3 mile into trail from Doudy Draw parking lot. Restrooms and picnic tables are available at Mesa Trail parking lot across the street from Doudy Draw parking lot. The only facility available at the Flatirons Vista parking lot is a medium size corral for horses. Your horses can drink water from the streams along the Doudy Draw Trail. Bring water for yourself.

Difficulty: Easy (Flatiron Vista Trail) to Moderate (Doudy Draw Trail)

Length of Trail: 6.8 miles round trip (can be longer, see Description)

Trail Usage: Horseback riding, hiking, bikes are permitted from the Doudy Trail parking lot and only on designated trails. Bikes are not allowed on the Doudy Draw Trail beyond the Community Ditch Trail. Dogs are permitted on a leash.

Directions: From its intersection with Baseline Road in Boulder, follow Broadway/CO 93 south for 4 miles to Eldorado Springs Drive/CO 170. Turn west (right) onto Eldorado Springs Drive/CO 170 traveling 2 miles to the Doudy Draw Trailhead parking lot which is on the south (left) side of the road.
To reach the Flatirons Vista Trailhead parking lot, continue further south on CO 93 from Eldorado Springs Drive/CO 170 for another 2.2 miles. The trailhead is on the west (right) side of the highway.
Both trailheads are well marked.

Flatirons Vista parking lot

Doudy Draw parking lot

First .3 mile is paved, I suggest that you ride off to the side on the dirt path (Doudy Draw)

Picnic area and restrooms (Doudy Draw)

Wooden bridge to cross, trail is well marked (Doudy Draw)

Pass through gate; be sure to close it behind you (Doudy Draw)

Cross a small stream, follow trail signs (Doudy Draw)

At 1.5 miles, fence line with choice of right or left. Doudy Draw Trail is to the left, right is an open space area for another day.

Cross another stream and start to climb (Doudy Draw)

Trail is narrower and rocky (Doudy Draw)

Lengthy set of stairs that climb past a wooden wall (Doudy Draw)

Wooden retaining wall by the stairs (Doudy Draw)

Trail continues to climb through pines to the top (Doudy Draw)

Through gate and meet what I will call the Flatiron Vista Trail

**At the top of the draw is a good place to let your
horse munch and rest**

Starting the trail from the Flatirons Vista parking lot (Flatirons)

Trail widens allowing "side-by-side" riding (Flatirons Vista)

Be sure to close any gate you open (Flatirons Vista)

Poles used for erosion control (Flatirons Vista)

Colorado at its finest!! (Flatirons Vista)

Power lines along the trail (Flatirons Vista)

At this "Y", continue to the right (Flatirons Vista)

End of the Flatirons Vista portion of the trail. (Flatirons Vista)

What a beautiful view !!!!! (Flatirons Vista)

General Information: If you are looking for fantastic views as well as a variety to your trails, this area is the place to be. This trail can be ridden in 3 different patterns:

1. From either parking lot, ride the Flatirons and Doudy DrawTrails from parking lot to parking lot and back. (Approximately 8 miles)

2. From the Doudy Draw parking lot, ride the Doudy DrawTrail to the top where it meets the Flatirons Trail and return to the Doudy Draw parking lot. (Approximately 4 miles)

3. From the Doudy Draw parking lot, ride the Doudy Draw trail to the gate that opens up to an open space to the west. This trail you will not find on a map. We rode for about a mile and turned around, not sure if it was OK to ride here. Later, we were told by a Ranger that it was open to equestrians. A trail for another time!!! (Mileage unknown)

I would consider the Doudy Draw Trail to be a moderate trail, needing shoes and mostly a "head-to-tail." Your horse will have bridges to cross, running streams and various sets of "steps." The set of steps that climb up the draw can be challenging in both directions with very little space to move off the trail. You will have a general climb with switchbacks, passing through another fence as you climb to the top. Take the time to enjoy the view of Boulder Valley. This is not a trail for a green horse or rider or a horse that is out of shape.

At the gate where you would start your descent into Doudy Draw, you will notice trails that go off to the south. Even though signs are not present, these are not "official" trails. As of this writing, a study is being conducted by the City of Boulder regarding this area.

Riding the trail from the Flatirons/Vista parking lot up to the gate prior to descending into Doudy Draw would be considered an easy trail. The elevation you gain is moderate and very gradual with plenty of space to ride "side-by-side" with lots of space on either side of the trail. Shoes for your horse are not needed here. I believe your horse should have shoes when riding into Doudy Draw. Expect to meet hikers and runners as well as livestock which may be in the various meadows. During winter months, check with the City of Boulder Parks & Recreation for trail conditions.

Notes:

MAP:

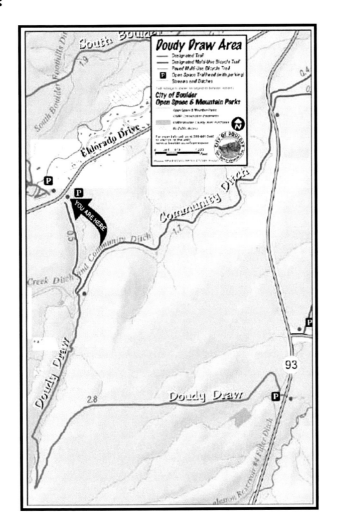

National Geographic #100
Or
City of Boulder Official Open Space & Mountain Parks Trails map
2002   (303-441-3440)

*"A horse can lend its rider the speed and strength he or she lacks,
but the rider who is wise remembers it is no more than a loan."*
–Pam Brown

Trail #17
Trail Name:

White Ranch (Jefferson)

Govt. Organization: Jefferson County Open Space (303) 271-5925

Fees: None

Beginning Elevation: 7,528 ft.

Ending Elevation: 8,000 ft.

Trailer Parking: Designated trailer parking at 2nd parking lot at west side of park, 6-8 trailers. 1st parking lot on west side of park is small, just off the road and will handle 1-2 trailers. Parking lot at east entrance of park will handle 6-8 trailers. The trail coming out of this parking lot climbs 1,200' in a 1 ½ mile stretch. Unless your horse is in extremely good shape and you are an experienced rider, I would suggest that horses start from the west side of park.

Facilities: Restrooms and water are at the 2nd parking lot at west side of park. Picnic tables with barbecue grates and a corral for your horses is also available.
East side of park at the parking lot offers picnic tables and restrooms.

Difficulty: Easy to moderate, depending on the trail

Length of Trail: Over 19 miles of trails

Trail Usage: Horseback riding, hiking, camping, and biking
Dogs are permitted on a leash.

Camping: Yes, Sourdough Springs Equestrian Camp. Must pack all camping items 2 miles to camp site. Water and restrooms are available at campsite. Each site has a hitching rail, picnic table and fire grate. Two 16 X 16 corrals, located "side-by-side," are available on a first come, first serve basis. Camping permits (advance and on-site) are free. Call Jefferson County Open Space for additional information.

White Ranch (Continued)

Directions: West Access trailhead (Gilpin County): Take CO 93 north from Golden approximately 1 mile to Golden Gate Canyon Road. Turn west (left) and travel 4.1 miles to Crawford Gulch Road (CR 57). Turn north (right) and travel approximately 4 miles to Belcher Hill Road. Turn east (right) and follow the signs to White Ranch, approximately 1 ½ miles. Parking is on the north (left) side of road. Best parking is in the second parking lot. Be careful not to drive past the entrance. The road goes to a dead end and you will probably have to back your trailer up a short but steep grade to the entrance of the parking lot. The roads to this trailhead are steep and very tight and winding, be sure your hauling vehicle is up to the drive.

East Access trailhead: Take CO 93 north from Golden 1.7 miles to west 56th Avenue. Turn west (left) on Pine Ridge Road and continue about 1 mile to the east parking lot. Do not use this lot if you are camping at the Sourdough Springs Equestrian Camp.

West side of park, 1st parking lot

West side of park, 2nd parking lot is the suggested area for entering trails with horses

Restrooms and hand pump for water (need muscles for this one!!)

Corral for your horses south of the picnic tables

We chose to start the Rawhide Trail on east side of parking lot

Trail is well marked

Black rubber on landscaping timber may be an obstacle for your horse

Exposed roots on trail, a possible shoe catcher

Trail became steep and extremely rocky

Another interesting spot on the trail, you might want to walk it

Trail hugs the side of the mountain for a short distance

Majority of the trail will be "head-to-tail" riding

One of the four equestrian camping spots

Corrals at the equestrian camping area

From the equestrian camp back to the trailhead, this portion
of the trail allows a little cantering

Back to parking lot and the camp sign-in sheet

We crossed the road and took the Sawmill Trail

Trail starts out "head-to-tail" with great views of Denver skyline

Trail widens for a short distance allowing "side-by-side" riding

At intersection, follow the Belcher Hill Trail towards the hiker campground

Trail stays wide into and through campground allowing "side-by-side" riding

Trail becomes rocky and you are back to riding "head-to-tail"

We took the Mustang Trail to the north, heading back to the parking lot.

Trail is under construction, this may become an obstacle for your horse

Trail is rocky with many switchbacks

Here we picked up Belcher Hill Trail and started down the mountain

189

Trail winds its way down toward the west side of White Ranch 1st parking lot

View from the Belcher Hill Trail of the 1st parking lot on the west side of White Ranch Park

Ride the road to the trailer at the 2nd parking lot

**Take the time to check out the antique farm equipment
at the west side of the park's 2nd parking lot**

General Information: We chose to ride the ranch from the west access 2nd parking lot. The drive to the lot was steep with tight curves, so make sure your vehicle is up to the climb. Be sure not to miss the entrance to the 2nd parking lot on your left. We did and had to back our trailer up a steep incline to the only entrance. The Rawhide Trail has two possible entrance points from the parking lot. Use the west entrance if you are packing into the Sourdough Springs Equestrian Camp, approximately 2 miles in. If you're camping, don't forget to sign in at the start of this entry. We took the east entry, knowing that it would be more rugged and we chose to ride it with a fresh horse.

I would consider the east side of Rawhide Trail to be a moderate trail. It is a steep climb, very rocky, exposed tree roots and at one point, hugs the edge of the mountain with "head-to-tail" riding. At the intersection of Waterhole Trail and Rawhide Trail, we took the Waterhole Trail to the equestrian campground. The trail was wide and allowed "side-by-side" riding. The campground was well designed for equestrians by including water, restrooms, hitching rails at each site as well as a two-stall 16 x16 corral. The corral is a first come, first gets. Traveling through the camp area, the trail intersects with the Rawhide Trail again. Taking the trail to the left, we rode the Rawhide Trail back to our trailer. This portion of the trail can easily be ridden with a green horse or beginner rider. The trail is used as a Service Road to the campground and is wide enough without major rocks to allow a good canter.

Back at the trailer we crossed the entrance road and picked up Sawmill Trail. The trail starts out to the east as a "head-to-tail" with great views of the city of Denver on a clear day. It widens for a short period allowing you to ride "side-by-side." At the first intersection we took the Belcher Hill Trail (according to the sign) toward the hiking campground. I believe it was really the Sawmill Trail. The trail to and through the campground was wide and allowed "side-by-side" riding. Up to this point, I believe a beginner horse or inexperienced rider could travel this portion of the Sawmill Trail. On the west side of the campground the trail becomes narrow again, rocky and more challenging. At the next intersection we turned right (north) on the Maverick Trail, heading back to the west entrance 1st parking lot.

The Maverick Trail climbed, was rocky and had multiple areas of steps that were still under construction. At the next intersection, we continued north on the Belcher Hill Trail, riding down the mountain to the 1st parking lot. From here, the access road to White Ranch becomes the trail to the parking lot and our trailer. White Ranch Park can become very busy on the weekends with bikers and hikers. We rode on a Monday and met very few people. Shoes are a must. The park is open all year, but for winter riding I would call for conditions. Pack a lunch and after your ride, put your horse in the corral and enjoy a picnic along with the great views. This was a great ride! I'm definitely coming back and I'm looking forward to riding the trails on the east side of the park.

Notes:

MAP:

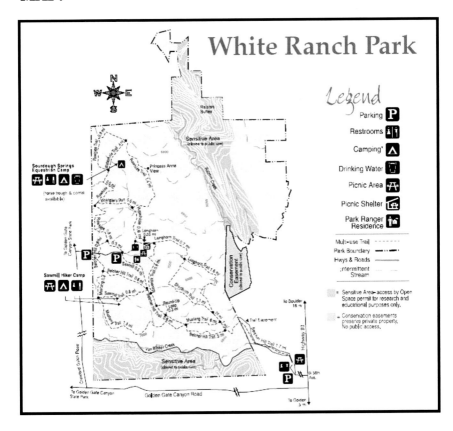

National Geographic Map #100

"Rider and horse must meet with joy and part as friends. The friendly greeting, the patting hand should never be absent when mounting and dismounting."
–F. V. Krane

Trail #18

Trail Name:

Caribou Ranch (Boulder)

Govt. Organization: Boulder County Parks & Open Space

Fees: None

Beginning Elevation: 8,344 ft.

Ending Elevation: 8,727 ft.

Trailer Parking: Parking for horses is at the Mud Lake parking lot only. Plenty of parking, no designated horse trailer area. Mud Lake parking lot is still under construction at the time of this writing.

Facilities: Port-a-potties at Mud Lake and Caribou parking lots. Restrooms are still under construction. Bring water for you and your horse.

Difficulty: Easy

Length of Trail: 4.2 miles roundtrip from the Caribou Trailhead. An additional mile roundtrip from the Mud Lake parking lot to the Caribou Trailhead.

Trail Usage: Horseback riding, hiking
Dogs are NOT permitted.

Directions: From Nederland travel north on CO 72 (Peak-to-Peak Highway) for about 1 mile. Turn west (left) onto CR 126, a dirt road, until you see the sign for the Mud Lake parking lot. Turn south (left) and travel approximately ¼ mile to parking lot. Park horse trailers on the upper portion of the lot. Note that the parking lot was under construction at the time of this writing.

NOTE: Caribou Ranch is closed annually from April 1st through June 30 to protect spring migratory birds and elk calving and rearing.

Turn left and park at the Mud Lake parking lot

Parking at the top lot at Mud Lake

We took the roads to the Caribou Ranch trailhead

Trail from the Mud Lake parking lot to the Caribou Ranch trailhead

The Delonde Trail starts out winding through pine forests

The Delonde Trail also meanders through meadows

Trail is well marked. Take the Blue Bird Loop to the Homestead as well as the "Blue Bird Mine"

Check out the Delonde Homestead

Have lunch at the Delonde Homestead and enjoy the beautiful views

The buildings at the Delonde Homestead are still being restored

Shoes are a necessity for your horse

I don't believe this was meant to be used by horses

Follow the signs to the "Blue Bird Mine"

Could it be that Sonny is asking Gem if she wants to race??

**The Mud Lake Trail back to parking lot is west of the
Caribou Trailhead**

The Mud Lake Trail is single file, mostly dirt with switch backs

Now this is an interesting "sculpture" along the Mud Lake Trail

Here we are back at the Mud Lake parking lot

General Information: What a fantastic trail!! This is a new trail that opened on October 15, 2004. Even though there is a parking lot at the Caribou Ranch Trailhead, it is for cars only. Please follow the signs and park at the Mud Lake parking lot. From the parking lot you can travel the road to the Caribou Trailhead or take the trail located at the northeast corner of the Mud Lake parking lot. The trail is well marked, fairly level, with some small climbs, and winds through large open meadows and stands of aspen and ponderosa trees. Follow the Delonde Trail for 1.2 miles and you will come to the Blue Bird Loop. We took the trail to the right (east). Pack a lunch and stop at the Delonde Homestead at the picnic table by the pond for an enjoyable view as well as a quick bite. When we were there, the house and barn were still being renovated. Ride past the homestead for about ¼ mile and you will see a steep set of steps that go down to a mountain stream. Even though there wasn't a sign saying that you couldn't take your horse down the steps, I don't believe it was meant to be used by horses. Continue along the trail a little bit further to the turn off on your right to the Blue Bird Mine. Be sure to read about the history associated with the mine. Retrace your steps and continue on your way using the Blue Bird Loop. This part of the trail opens up into a large meadow. As we let our horses eat, it was easy to imagine the ranchers of yesteryear cutting and baling the hay. The trail here is wide and just beckons you to gallop your horse. Continuing on the Blue Bird Loop, the trail ties back into the Delonde Trail and back to the Caribou Ranch Trailhead. Instead of going back on the road, we chose to ride the Mud Lake trail back to the Mud Lake parking lot. This trail is west of the Caribou Ranch trailhead across the road. The trail meanders with small switch backs, through trees back to the parking lot. Check out the "sculpture." This trail also intersects with the Mud Lake Open Space Trails. This will be more trails to ride and document for a future book. We rode this on a Sunday and encountered very few people. I'm sure this won't last long once the word gets around how beautiful the trail is. I would ride this trail with a green horse or a beginning rider. It's a good first "mountain ride." Shoes are needed. This is definitely a trail to ride again.

Notes:

MAP:

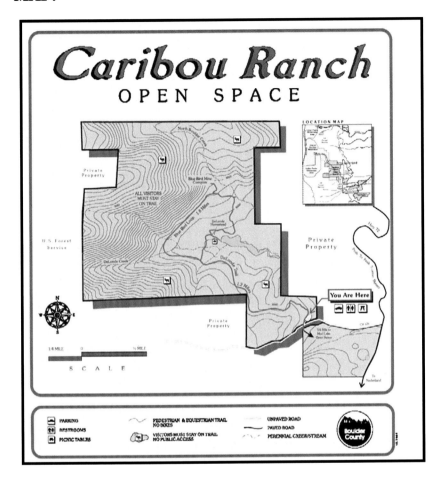

National Geographic Map #100

"Good saddles ain't cheep, and cheap saddles ain't good."
–Cowboy Proverb

Trail #19
Trail Name:

Bear Creek Lake Park (Jefferson)

Govt. Organization: City of Lakewood (303) 697-6159

Fees: Yes, $4 at time of this writing

Beginning Elevation: 5,558 ft.

Ending Elevation: 5,779 ft.

Trailer Parking: Plenty of parking, park at Whitetail, Cottontail or Muskrat Meadows lots, although the Ranger prefers you park at Whitetail. Between the 3 lots, 10 to 15 trailer spaces are available.

Facilities: Port-a-potties, covered picnic areas, water, grills. Water is available for your horse along the trail.

Difficulty: Easy to moderate

Length of Trail: 9 miles roundtrip

Trail Usage: Horseback riding, hiking, fishermen, boaters
Dogs are permitted on a leash.

Directions: From I 25, take I 76 west which will link together with I 70. Exit onto C 470 south/east and travel to the Morrison Road Exit. Turn east (left) traveling for approximately ¼ mile to the entrance of the park which will be on the south (right) side of the road. From the northwest outskirts of Loveland, it was approximately 68 miles one way.

Parking at the Cottontail lot

Trail starts at the southeast corner of parking lot

Trail is well marked as to where horses are "not" permitted

Sign at this entry point allowed horses to cross this stream

Trail passes through meadows and wooded areas

Trail skirts a horse rental stable in the park (303) 697-9666

Various places, the trail will cross the park road

Portions of the trail allow for "side-by-side" riding.

Starting the climb on Mt. Carbon, "head-to-tail"

View from Mt. Carbon, Denver skyline to the east and a golf course behind the horse and rider

Heading down Mt. Carbon toward the dam

Trail skirts a golf course

Trail passes by the maintenance building

Crossing a cement "bridge" with the park road on your left

Riding along Morrison Road

Parking lot at Whitetail

Trail is mostly dirt with a few rocks, this horse rode barefoot

Trails are marked by number/letters making it confusing when trying to match the trail names on the map

General Information: I never would have imagined that a beautiful park like Bear Creek Lake Park would reside just off a major highway like C 470. This park has the potential for an easy to moderate ride depending on what trails you take. At the park entrance, pay your $4 fee, pick up your map and ask the Ranger which of the three lots (Cottontail, Muskrat Meadows and Whitetail) would be the best to park at for your particular ride. After leaving the park entrance the road forks. Take the left fork to get to the various parking lots. As we started our ride, we noticed that most trail signs did not match what was on the trail map!! In order to know where we were, we used the landmarks on the map to help guide us (Big Soda Lake, Camp Area, Stables, Reservoir, Mt. Carbon, etc.). The trail is mostly dirt, a little rocky in spots, with a few crossings over the paved park road. I believe that the water crossings, the trail coming down Mt. Carbon which passes the golf course and maintenance buildings as well as paralleling a portion of Morrison Road would make this a moderate trail. What's nice about the park is if your horse is not ready for these obstacles, you can plan your ride to bypass them. This would then make it an "easy" trail. The various trails range from riding "side-by-side" to "head-to-tail" amid meadows, wooded areas and along ponds. I would suggest sunscreen, hats and bug spray in the hot months. The park is open year round but it would be good to call to check trail conditions in the winter months. We rode in the early spring and one water crossing on this trail was fairly wide and deep with rushing water forceful enough that it did push our horses a little down stream. Another water crossing that we encountered was a lot easier. Again, know your horse's limits. If you ride up Mt. Carbon, check out the views. On a clear day you will be able to see the skyline of Denver to your east. When we rode down the east side of Mt. Carbon, my horse was a little wary of the golfers and their carts. I mention this because the trail down is narrow and a little steep and could become a problem if your horse has troubles with these sights and sounds. We rode on a Wednesday but I would assume the park would be busier on the weekends, especially during the summer months. There is plenty of parking and the park is laid out so that it should be able to handle the volume.

Notes:

MAP:

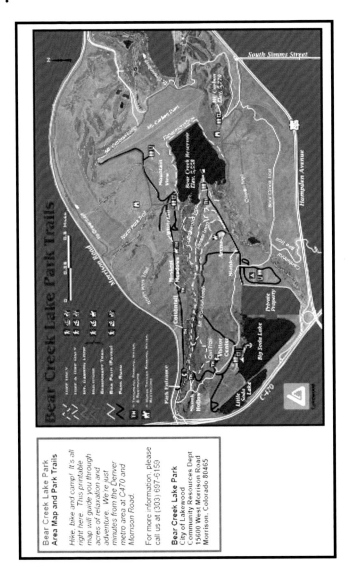

National Geographic Map #100

"A horse is the projection of people's dreams about themselves; strong, powerful, beautiful and it has the capability of giving us escape from our mundane existence."
–Pam Brown

218

Trail #20
Trail Name:
Golden Gate Canyon State Park (Gilpin/Jefferson)

Govt. Organization: Colorado State Parks (303) 582-3707

Fees: Yes, $5 per vehicle, purchase at Visitor Center or self service stations.

Beginning Elevation: 7,400

Ending Elevation: 10,300

Trailer Parking: Nott Creek parking lot, 5 trailer spaces, trail access is to the west of lot
Kriley Pond parking lot, 3 trailer spaces, trail access to the east of lot

Camping: Yes, reservations needed at Aspen Meadow Campground #22 and #23. There are no corrals, bring your own panels, trailer tie or high line tie Restroom, dumpster and water pump Permit fee is $12 + daily park entry fee of $5

Facilities: Restrooms, picnic tables, water pumps at various trailheads

Difficulty: Moderate and Difficult depending on trail

Length of Trail: 22 miles, made up of various trails

Trail Usage: Horseback riding, hiking, camping, biking, hunting and picnics
Dogs are permitted on a leash.

Directions: To get to Golden Gate, take CO 93 north from Golden 1 mile to Golden Gate Canyon Road. Turn west (left) and continue 15 miles to the park. Stop at Ranger Station to pay fee, get map and directions to various parking lots for horse trailers.

Parking at the Aspen Meadow Campground in order to ride the west side of Golden Gate Canyon State Park

Started the trail toward Dude's Fishing Hole in order to catch the Mule Deer Trail

Hopefully, this has been repaired

Trails are well marked

An exposed culvert to walk over

Typical mountain trail of dirt and rocks

Watch for exposed tree roots in trail as you climb

Check out the Mule Deer footprint on the tree for trail marking

This portion of the trail allows "side-by-side" riding with few rocks

Riding past a small pond, the trail was a little water logged here

A shelter that would have been helpful during the hail storm we encountered toward the end of our ride

Backcountry campsites at Greenfield Meadow

Passing an old cabin, trail is embedded with wood for erosion control

Small bridge to cross near the cabin

Descending via switchbacks into a valley

Check out the view as you descend into the valley

Into the valley we travel (notice the black clouds starting to form!!!)

Across a park road, heading toward Ole' Barn Knoll

Over a bridge and through a meadow

Up a set of steps, still out in the open with a storm brewing

Over another bridge and back into the trees

Another bridge to cross and still a mile or so to the trailer

**On the Elk Trail, heading toward Panorama Point,
now it's raining**

**After waiting out the rain/hail storm, finally made it back
to the Aspen Meadows Campground**

General Information: Only 30 miles west of Denver, Golden Gate Canyon State Park consists of 12,000 acres and over 22 miles of various trails ranging from moderate to difficult. These are definitely mountain trails and you will need a vehicle that can pull steep grades and handle tight switch backs. Upon our arrival at the park we stopped at the Visitors Center for our daily pass, map, and a quick orientation to the area. After talking with the Rangers about the various trails, we chose to ride the west side of the park. The Rangers suggested that we park at the Aspen Meadows Campground and start our ride there. Even though it was early June, sunny and clear, we were wearing jackets, carrying gloves and rain gear on our horses. One of the first things that we noticed was that the trail was marked with signs depicting various animal footprints. The trails, after all, were named after various animals. The trails were well marked with not only the footprints on trees but signs along the trail with the name as well as the footprint. This was helpful for me because I had trouble knowing a Mule Deer from an Elk print!! Shoes were definitely needed since the trail was moderately to very rocky in spots. Your horse needs to be in good shape to handle the gradual climb in elevation. Approximately 25% of the trail may be ridden "side-by-side." We rode through forests, meadows, past ponds, backcountry campgrounds and old cabins. Due to the wet spring, portions of the trail were a little boggy. Various forms of bridges were encountered in the meadows along the trail. The views as you descend toward Mt. Base Road are fantastic!! We found the ride to be extremely enjoyable up until the storm clouds started to move in.

We were about 2 miles from the end of the ride when we started to hear thunder in the distance. Needless to say, our speed picked up. To make a long story short, we spend almost ¾ hour in a rain/hail mountain storm. We were very fortunate that our horses handled the rain/hail, lightening and thunder extremely well.

These trails are mountain riding in Colorado at its best. These are definitely trails for an experienced horse as well as rider. Because of the elevation and length, horse and rider need to be in shape. Be sure that your horse is well shod. The park map, jacket, gloves, hat and raincoat are a must. With bears and mountain lions in the area, bells on at least one of the horses would be a good idea. If this is your first time at the park, talk with the Rangers to get a "feel for the land." This also lets the Rangers know where you will be riding. I plan to return and camp at the Aspen Meadows Campground in order to ride the eastern trails and the remaining western trails that we missed.

Notes:

MAP:

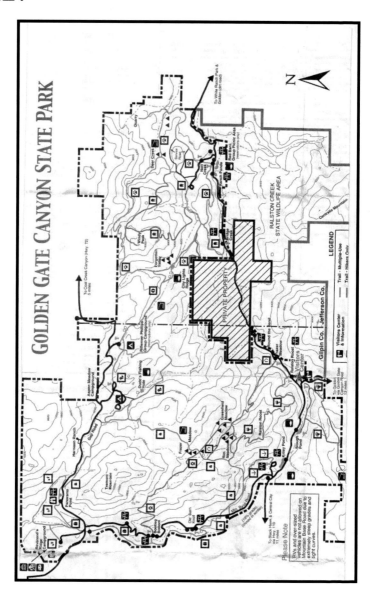

National Geographic Map #100

"Show me your horse and I will tell you what you are."
–Old English Saying

Trail #21
Trail Name:

Indiana Equestrian Center (Jefferson)

Govt. Organization: City of Arvada Parks & Recreation (720) 898-7392

Fees: None

Beginning Elevation: 5,300 ft.

Ending Elevation: 5,300 ft.

Trailer Parking: Parking easily accommodates large trailers with ample room to maneuver. Gravel lot will accommodate 15 – 20 trailers.

Facilities: Large arena with spectator stands, port-a-potty, picnic tables, water pump near box stalls for horses. Riders bring your own water.

Difficulty: Easy

Length of Trail: 2 mile roundtrip dirt trail around facilities

Trail Usage: Horseback riding, hiking
Dogs are permitted on a leash.

Directions: From I 70, exit onto Ward Road (in Arvada). Proceed north on Ward Road to Ralston Road (64th Ave.) Turn west (left) on Ralston Road (64th Ave.) to Indiana Street. Turn north (right) on Indiana Street traveling to about 76th Ave., just past the small white church on the east (right) side of the road.

Entrance to the Indiana Equestrian Center

Large parking lot

235

Restroom facilities

Water is to the north of these box stalls

**Practice opening gates and getting your mail
or use the open arena**

Trail, wide enough for "side-by-side" riding, circles area

A well constructed round pen

Arena with spectator stands

General Information: This is an excellent location to bring a green horse or green rider to expose them to various obstacles that one may find on a trail. A rider can practice opening gates and approaching the scary "mail box" in a safe environment. The loop around the Equestrian Center is a perfect place for your 1st trail ride. The round pen, arena and other facilities make this a very horse friendly environment. In the winter, this would be an excellent site to get away from the barn and give you and your horse some exercise. This center is used by various horse clubs for events during the year. Check with the City of Arvada Parks & Recreation if concerned about what might be going on at any particular time.

Notes:

MAP:

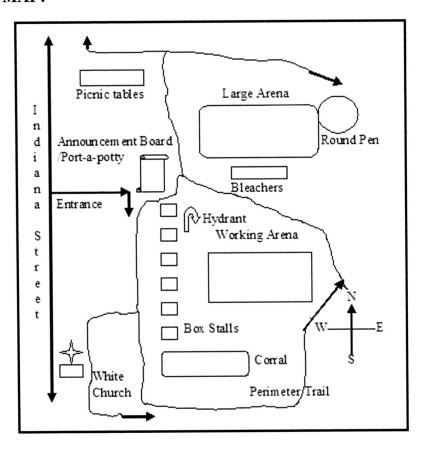

"We gaze upon their quiet beauty, their natural elegance, and we are captivated. They see us softly, in gentle light....rewarding human companionship with strength, grace and intelligence. As they run through arenas and open fields, past mountains and seas, moving like the wind toward heaven, we travel with them, if only in our hearts."
-Anonymous

Trail #22
Trail Name:

South Valley Park (Jefferson)

Govt. Organization: Jefferson County Open Space – (303) 271-5925

Fees: None

Beginning Elevation: 5,954 ft.

Ending Elevation: 6,260 ft.

Trailer Parking: North parking lot – Main parking lot with room for 4-5 trailers

South parking lot – Smaller lot with room for 3-4 trailers

Facilities: Restrooms and picnic tables at each parking lot. Bring water for horse and rider

Difficulty: Easy (One road crossing if riding Grazing Elk Trail)

Length of Trail: 5.5 miles roundtrip on Coyote Song Trail & Grazing Elk Trail loop

Trail Usage: Horseback riding, hiking
Dogs are permitted on a leash.

Directions: From I 70 exit on C 470 traveling south/east. Exit west (right) on Ken Caryl Ave. traveling for approximately ¼ mile. Turn south (left) onto South Valley Road traveling approximately 2 miles. Turn northeast (left) into the park's North parking lot (main lot).

If coming from the south using C 470, exit onto S. Wadsworth Blvd./CO 121 heading south for approximately ¼ mile. Turn west (right) on South Deer Creek Canyon Road and travel for approximately 2.5 miles. Turn north (right) into the South parking lot.

North parking lot (main lot)

South parking lot off of South Valley Road

Coyote Song Trail starts at the south parking area

Trail is a "head-to-tail" up and down small hills and occasionally through trees and brush

Rock formations that remind one of a small "Garden of the Gods"

Lockheed Martin can be viewed off to the west

Traveling south for .4 mile will eventually bring you to the South parking lot and the end of the trail

At same junction, travel west for .5 mile to a private road to continue to Grazing Elk Trail

Passing the south end of the Swallow Trail (hiking only)

Trail passes through a small marshy area

In order to continue to Grazing Elk Trail, you need to cross this road. Be careful, at times the road can be busy.

Trails are well marked

Climbing a small grade to the meadow at the top

Grazing Elk Trail is a 2.2 mile loop. This is the end of South Valley Park. Retrace your steps back to your trailer.

Rattlesnake Gulch Trail at south end of Grazing Elk Trail will take you to Deer Canyon Park (see Trail #23)

Returning to our trailer at the north parking lot at South Valley Park

General Information: We started our ride from the north parking lot at South Valley Road. The Coyote Song Trail and the Swallow Trail both started at the east end of the lot. I don't know if we just missed seeing the signs or if it just wasn't well marked, because at first we weren't sure if we were on the correct trail. Pretending to be trackers, we took the trail that had hoof prints. A short distance down the trail we found a sign letting us know that we had chosen correctly and were on the Coyote Song Trail. The trails are dirt with minimal rocks and fantastic views. The rock formations along the way reminded me of the "Garden of the Gods" in Colorado Springs. At approximately .5 mile along Coyote Song Trail, the Lyon's Back Trail branches off to the left (east) and connects to the Ken-Caryl Ranch Foundation. This area is covered in Trail #24. Continuing on the Coyote Song Trail, at approximately 1 mile, you will encounter a "Y." This "Y" is not marked with the name of a trail, just the symbol ←→. We decided to continue straight and after another .5 mile we found ourselves at the south parking lot on Deer Creek Canyon Road. Turning around we went back to the spot where the trail came to a "Y" and took the left (west) fork. After .2 mile we encountered the south end of the Swallow Trail. Continuing, we rode through a marshy area and after another .3 mile we were at the private road that is the entrance to Lockheed-Martin. We crossed the road and continued on the Grazing Elk Trail. This trail climbs .3 mile up to the meadow and a 2.2 mile loop. This trail may be closed when elk populations in the valley are high. If you plan to ride the Grazing Elk Trail, I would suggest you call the Jefferson County Open Space for an update. On the far south side of the loop, you'll find Rattlesnake Gulch Trail which connects you to Deer Creek Canyon Park. This trail will be covered in Trail #23. If you ride the trails described here, shoes are not required. Winter riding is feasible, call ahead for conditions. I believe this trail could be ridden with a green horse and an advanced beginner rider. Expect the trail to be busy with hikers, bikers and bird watchers. We rode on a Wednesday and met quite a few people bird watching and hiking. We were the only users of the Grazing Elk Trail. During sunny weather, bring a hat and sun screen. There is very little shade on the trails.

Notes:

MAP:

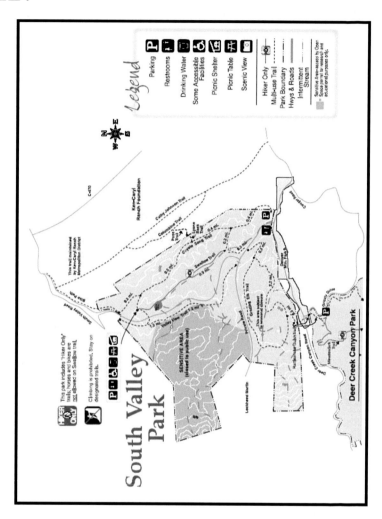

National Geographic Map #100

"I pray that gentle hands May guide my feet;
I ask for kind commands From voices sweet;
At night a stable warm With scented hay,
Where, safe from every harm, I'll sleep till day."
–Pony's Prayer

Trail #23
Trail Name:

Deer Creek Canyon Park (Jefferson)

Govt. Organization: Jefferson County Open Space (303) 271-5925

Fees: None

Beginning Elevation: 6,116 ft.

Ending Elevation: 7,200 ft.

Trailer Parking: If parking at South Valley Park, see Trail #22
If parking at Deer Creek Canyon Park – 5-8 trailers

Facilities: Restrooms and picnic tables at each parking lot. Bring water for horse and rider

Difficulty: Moderate to Difficult

Length of Trail: 11 miles with two loops

Trail Usage: Horseback riding, hiking, biking
Dogs are permitted on a leash.

Directions: If parking at South Valley Park, see Trail #22

If parking at Deer Creek Canyon Park,
From C 470, exit onto S. Wadsworth Blvd./CO 121 heading south for approximately ¼ mile. Turn west (right) on South Deer Creek Canyon Road and travel for approximately 2.5 miles. Turn south (left) on Grizzly Drive and travel ¼ mile turning west (right) into Deer Creek Canyon Park. Note that Grizzly Drive is a steep grade into park.

North parking lot (main lot) – South Valley Park

South parking lot off of South Valley Road – South Valley Park

Parking at Deer Creek Canyon Park

Heading toward Deer Creek Canyon Park on Rattlesnake Gulch Trail off of Grazing Elk Trail in South Valley Park

Trail winds up and down small valleys

Small bridge to cross on Rattlesnake Gulch Trail

Crossing Deer Creek Road

**Cross a bridge and travel along road for a short distance
to pick up Rattlesnake Gulch Tail**

Trail continues to climb, paralleling Grizzly Drive

A good place to stop and have lunch before proceeding on Plymouth Creek Trail

The Plymouth Creek Trail is concrete for a short distance

Plymouth Creek Trail becomes dirt and we start our climb

**Expect to meet bikes as well as hikers along this trail.
Sometimes you may not have much of a warning.**

Trail is well marked

Trail becomes rockier and steeper the further along you go

You definitely want to get off and walk this section

A small mountain stream allowed us to give our horses a drink
and a much needed rest before we started to climb again.

We took the right fork on the trail

One of the three trails that are for hikers only

Red Mesa Loop is a 2.5 mile loop

General Information: The day that we rode South Valley Park (Trail #22) we decided to continue our ride into Deer Creek Canyon Park. We took the Rattlesnake Gulch Trail for almost 1 mile into Deer Creek Canyon Park. Shoes are a must for your horse on these trails. We wound our way up and down the trail, across a small bridge until we came to Deer Creek Canyon Road. Crossing the road, we continued on Grizzly Drive and over a small bridge until we picked up Rattlesnake Gulch Trail. We climbed the trail, paralleling Grizzly Drive and arrived at the parking lot and trailhead for Deer Creek Canyon Park. This portion of the trail is very narrow. It would be hard to find a spot to get off the trail if a bike came zipping around a corner. We made sure we kept talking in order to make ourselves a little more "visible." Picking up Plymouth Creek Trail from the parking lot, we continued to climb. Deer Creek Canyon Park has more elevation, is a lot rockier and has more bikes and hikers than South Valley Park. The trail is best ridden "head-to-tail" in order to accommodate the bikes that you will meet going up and down the trail. Be aware that there are quite a few blind spots where people going up or down the trail may not see you. This is where having bells on your horse is another benefit. One of the most challenging spots was the steps and the extremely rocky area next to them. The steps were too narrow and close together to ride or walk your horse on. Even walking with your horse over the rocks (in a lot of cases they could have been boulders) was challenging. Along the way, stop at the stream and give your horse the opportunity to get a drink and rest. The Red Mesa Loop had a scenic photo view of the canyon and forested sections. If you take the Plymouth Mountain Trail expect an even steeper climb.

This is a trail for an experienced horse and rider. Be sure your horse is in good shape and able to handle the climbing. The park is open year round but check for conditions if winter riding.

Notes:

MAP:

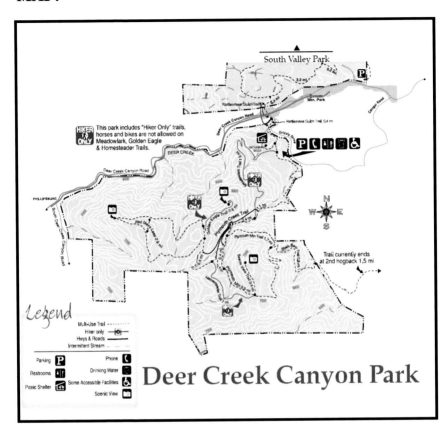

National Geographic Map #100

"Sell the cow, buy the sheep, but never be without the horse."
–Irish Proverb

264

Trail #24

Trail Name:

Ken-Caryl Ranch Foundation (Jefferson)

Govt. Organization: Ken-Caryl Ranch Metropolitan District (303) 979-7424

Fees: None

Beginning Elevation: 5,954 ft.

Ending Elevation: 6,260 ft.

Trailer Parking: North parking lot – Main parking lot with room for 4-5 trailers.

South parking lot – Smaller lot with room for 3-4 trailers.

Facilities: Restrooms and picnic tables at each parking lot. Bring water for horse and rider

Difficulty: Easy – Moderate (Lyon's Back Trail & Pass Trail)

Length of Trail: 5 miles roundtrip

Trail Usage: Horseback riding, hiking, biking
Dogs are permitted on a leash.

Directions: From I 70 exit on C 470 traveling south/east. Exit west (right) on Ken Caryl Ave. traveling for approximately ¼ mile. Turn south (left) onto South Valley Road traveling approximately 2 miles. Turn northeast (left) into the park's North parking lot (main lot).

If coming from the south, using C 470, exit S. Wadsworth Blvd./CO 121 heading south for approximately ¼ mile. Turn west (right) on South Deer Creek Canyon Road and travel for approximately 2.5 miles. Turn right (north) onto S. Valley Road. The South parking lot will be on the right (east) side.

North parking lot (main lot) – South Valley Park

South parking lot off of South Valley Road

Coyote Song Trail starts at the south parking area

Take the Lyon's Back Trail that veers off of the Coyote Song Trail

Trail starts to climb through thickets

Rock steps

This portion of the trail is all one big rock

Steps to maneuver

Trail becomes less rocky

Entering Ken-Caryl Foundation Open Space

**Continuing straight takes you to the Cathy Johnson Trail.
The right takes you along the Columbine Trail**

Columbine Trail winds through brush and small trees

The foliage gets a little thick in places

Coming down to meet the Cathy Johnson Trail

Trail is well marked

Cathy Johnson Trail allows you to ride "side-by-side"

Cathy Johnson Trailhead on South Valley Road

Riding along the bike path on South Valley Road

Continue past the lights

To the right just beyond the light, pick up the Coyote Song Trail back to the main parking lot at South Valley Park

General Information: We rode South Valley Park, Deer Creek Canyon Park and the trails at the Ken-Caryl Foundation all in one day. We picked up the Lyon's Back Trail off Coyote Song Trail. Lyon's Back Trail gradually picks up some elevation, heading out of South Valley Park. With the elevation, rockier footing and rock steps, this portion of the trail becomes challenging. On the other side of these obstacles the trail becomes dirt again with much improved footing.

Entering into the Ken-Caryl Open Space, you have the choice of going down to meet the Cathy Johnson Trail immediately or traveling parallel to it on the Columbine Trail. We chose the Columbine Trail because it looked to be more interesting. The Columbine Trail winds up and down the side of the hill, sometimes through thickets and other times through open space. It eventually comes down and meets up with the Cathy Johnson Trail.

The Cathy Johnson Trail stretches from the South Valley Road to the Deer Creek Canyon Road. It's approximately 4 miles round trip. We chose to continue left (north) toward the South Valley Road and find our way back to the parking lot at South Valley Park. At South Valley Road, we turned left (west) and rode along a bike trail for approximately ¾ mile. Beyond the light we were able to pick up the Coyote Song Trail that took us back to the parking lot at South Valley Park. If a person wanted to just ride the Cathy Johnson Trail, you could leave from the South Valley Park main lot, travel along the bike path to the Cathy Johnson Trail and ride the trail to the Deer Creek Canyon Road and back. This way you would bypass all of the rocks and climbing and the only obstacle would be the traffic along South Valley Road.

If you are just riding the Cathy Johnson Trail, shoes are not needed. Again this is an open area and sunscreen and a hat would be appropriate. Rattlesnakes and mountain lions are active in this area.

Notes:

MAP:

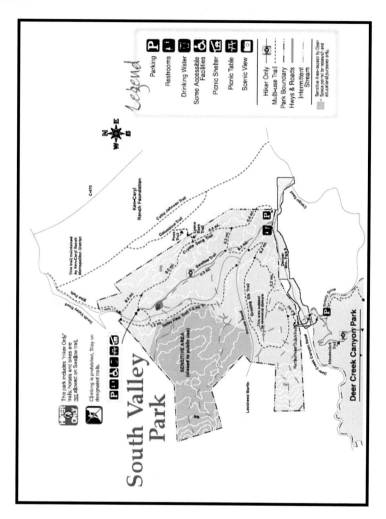

National Geographic Map #100

"A horseman should know neither fear nor anger."
–James Reary

Trail #25
Trail Name:

Chatfield State Park (Jefferson)

Govt. Organization: Colorado State Parks, Chatfield (303) 791-7275

Fees: $5 Day after Labor Day through April 30
$6 Day May 1 through Labor Day

Beginning Elevation: 5,470 ft.

Ending Elevation: 5,470 ft.

Trailer Parking: Designated parking lot for 15 to 20 horse trailers.

Facilities: Rest rooms at various parking lots Visitor Center in the park Water is available for your horse by the public corrals. You may also water your horse in the southern point of the South Platte River. Bring water for yourself.

Camping: Visitors may leave their horses in the corrals overnight if they are camping in the campground, two miles from the corrals. Visitors must furnish their own feed, as grazing is not allowed and hydrants are at the corrals. For additional information on camping sites for you, call the Chatfield Park Office at (303) 791-7275.

Difficulty: Easy

Length of Trail: 3.2 miles Equestrian Loop, 25 miles of trails, not all are accessible to horses.

Trail Usage: Horseback riding, hiking, biking
Dogs are permitted on a leash.

Chatfield State Park (Continued)

Directions: From south Denver, take C 470 west and exit at S. Wadsworth Blvd./CO 121 heading south. Continue to travel 1 mile to the Deer Creek Park entrance on the east (left) side of the road. Entering the park, the road will curve north to the Ranger Station then back to the east coming to a "T." Turn south (right) for ¼ mile. You will see a sign for the public stables which veers towards the right. Turn here (right) then continue traveling ¾ mile toward the public equestrian parking lot, which is the upper west lot. The lower lot belongs to the Chatfield Livery.

Equestrian public parking lot

Horses for rent at the Chatfield Stables

Corrals that can be used for overnight stays across from the equestrian parking lot

Close up view of the corrals for overnight stays

Restroom and water to the right (east) of the corrals

Portions of the trails allow "side-by-side" riding

South Platt River flows through the park

Portions of the trails are beside concrete paths

Campgrounds by reservations 2 miles from the horse corrals

Riders enjoying the park

General Information: Chatfield State Park is a very diversified area offering camping, a full-service livery, 25 miles of hiking and biking trails, a popular lake, the Chatfield marina, model airplane paved runways and one of the most popular hot-air balloon launch areas on the Front Range. Even though there are 25 miles of trails, not all are accessible to horses. Of all the trails and maps in this book, I found Chatfield to be the most confusing. The map does not show named trails and it was rare when I actually found a sign. Talking with a Ranger, I was told horses were to stay in the "center" of the park and to the southern end. Horses are prohibited at picnic sites, campsites and the swim beach. We found the western outer trails in the southern end of the park to be more of an open area and the inner trails to be more wooded. When we ride here again, I probably will make sure that I'm riding with someone who has been here before. We just rode around, looking for hoof prints or other horses.

The trails are dirt, shoes are not necessary. The trails are mostly flat with a few rolling hills. This is a very popular park, so expect to arrive early if you ride on weekends or holidays. Be careful if traveling along the paved road in the park, it can get very busy. As stated earlier, be prepared to hear noises and see sights from model airplanes, hot-air balloons and boats. Wildlife is plentiful in the park. White tail & mule deer, coyotes, muskrats, fox, beaver and numerous species of birds make their home here. The park is open year round. Call the park office for conditions for winter riding.

Notes:

MAP:

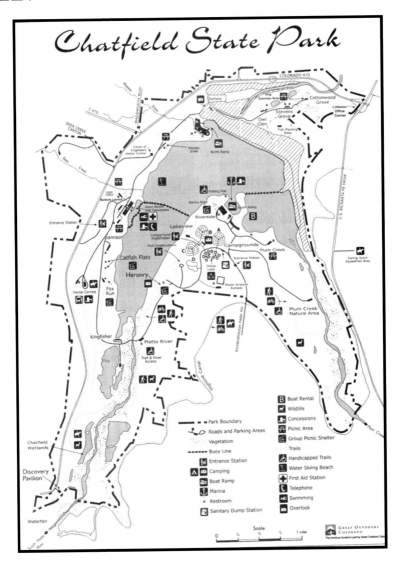

National Geographic Map #100

"A horse will go according as it is held by the bridle."
-Indian Proverb

Trail #26
Trail Name:

Indian Creek Equestrian Trail (Douglas)

Govt. Organization: Pike National Forest (303) 275-5610

Fees: Yes, Day use only is $4/day. See "Camping" for other fees.

Beginning Elevation: 7,412 ft.

Ending Elevation: 8,448 ft.

Trailer Parking: Main parking lot easily accommodates room for 12 or more trailers. There is ample room to maneuver.

Facilities: Restrooms & water at main parking lot

Camping: 7 campsites with spurs 50'-60' in length to accommodate horse trailers. Facilities include: water, tables, vault toilets, fire rings and hitching rails. User fees are $15/night. Make reservations for the equestrian campground by calling (877) 444-6777 or going online at www.reserveusa.com.

Difficulty: Moderate – Difficult

Length of Trail: 15 miles roundtrip

Trail Usage: Horseback riding, hiking, biking
Dogs are permitted on a leash.

Directions: Drive southwest from Denver on Santa Fe Dr (US 85) to Sedalia. Turn west (right) on Douglas CR 67. Drive slightly over 10 miles to the Indian Creek Campground. The parking lot is on the north (right) side of the road. The trailhead is just to the north (right) of the parking area. Be sure your hauling vehicle is able to handle mountain roads.

Day use parking lot

Parking at an equestrian camp site

We started at the trailhead just north (right) of the day use parking lot

Majority of trail is "head-to-tail" and rocky

Views are spectacular as you gradually climb

Trail meanders through some heavy oak thickets

**Trail widens and intersects with Ringtail & Sharptail Trail.
Stay on Indian Creek Trail (Pike National Forest #800)**

Continue to climb through an aspen area

Pass under high power lines

Descending into a valley

Entering Roxborough State Park, dogs are not permitted here

Trail becomes narrow and heavily wooded

Trail opens up into meadows for a short distance

Trail becomes very steep, narrow and rocky

Working our way back to the Indian Creek Campground

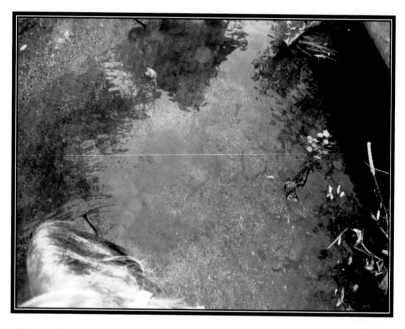

The only water we found was at Bear Creek, almost at the end of the 15 mile ride

Check out Mary's "new" hat!!

We emerged from the trail at the west end of the equestrian campground, one horseshoe lighter.

Emergency shoeing in Sedalia

Thank you Ed Bullock & Jason Hays for fitting us into your busy schedule.

General Information: We rode this trail at the end of September just in time for the fall colors. We started from the trailhead just north of the day use parking lot and made the loop from east to west. The trail started out well marked but soon the signs became few and far between. It also became confusing to find signs where the "horse" was weathered off the sign. Keep on the Indian Creek (Pike National Forest #800) trail.

At the beginning, the trail was narrow with "head-to-tail" riding. The views were spectacular as we wound our way up the mountain through the pines. At the intersection of Sharptail Trail and Ringtail Trail, the trail opened up, allowing "side-by-side" riding. After entering into Roxborough State Park, the trail became narrower and more wooded. Suddenly, the trail opened up into a large meadow. This was a good spot to rest our horses and let them munch on grass.

Continuing on the trail we came to a spot with signs for Waterton Trail and Waterton Loop but nothing for Indian Creek Trail. This was the most confusing spot on the trail for us. After talking with some bike riders and checking our map, we continued to the left (west) on the portion of the trail that was not noted on the sign. The trail then became very steep, narrow, and rocky with switchbacks and drop offs. The views were breathtaking though. Because of the use by bikers, this portion of the trail did make us a little nervous. The trail eventually widened but we continued to climb and move more away from the side of the mountain.

We were now about 10 miles into the trail and no water was to be found. All of the streams were dry. Even though our horses are in good shape, we did get off and walk after giving them water from our water bottles. First time I ever had my horse drink out of a water bottle!! Finally, the trail leveled off at the top and we slowly worked our way back down into the valley. At about 1 mile from the end of the trail, we were able to water our horses at Bear Creek. Another ¾ mile and my horse lost a front shoe.

Indian Creek – General Information (Continued)

This was a great ride but not for a green horse and rider or a horse that is not in shape for mountain trails. Talking to locals, I found that this trail usually has water available. In fact 2 weeks earlier, water was not a problem. I would consider 70% of the trail to be very rocky, narrow with switchbacks and places with major elevation gains. Be sure to carry a map with you. I called the South Platte Ranger District for mine at (303) 275-5610.

This is a very long, strenuous ride and a wrong turn could put you out of your way and riding beyond dusk. Be aware that there are social/unofficial trails that you will be crossing. Also, near the shoe that my horse lost, we did find mountain lion scat. Use bells on your horses for the animals as well as for letting the bikers and hikers know of your presence. Shoes are a must.

Notes:

MAP:

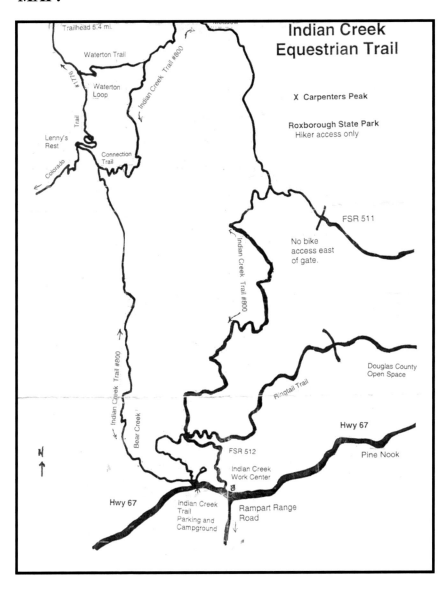

National Geographic Map #135

"The horse is God's gift to mankind."
–Arab Proverb

Trail #27
Trail Name:

Spruce Meadows Trail (Douglas)

Govt. Organization: Douglas County Open Space (303) 660-7495

Fees: No

Beginning Elevation: 6,950 ft.

Ending Elevation: 7,100 ft.

Trailer Parking: Main parking lot easily accommodates room for 20 or more trailers. There is ample room to maneuver.

Facilities: Port-a-potties and hitching rail at parking lot. Water is available at stock ponds along the trail and at nearby Greenland Open Space trailhead.

Difficulty: Easy - Moderate (Slippery grass surface trail, crosses Spruce Mountain Road twice and Noe Road twice at marked crossings, within sight and sound of active railroad tracks)

Length of Trail: 8.5 miles roundtrip

Trail Usage: Horseback riding, hiking, biking
Dogs are permitted on a leash.

Directions: From Denver take I 25 south to the Greenland Exit (#167). Turn west (right) and travel ¼ mile. The road will then jog to the south then continue for ½ mile. Bypass the Greenland Trailhead and continue to the west (right) on Noe Road (gravel road) over two sets of railroad tracks. The parking area is just up a short hill on the south (left) of the road.

Day use parking lot will handle "many" trailers

Port-a-potties and hitching rail

Trail is well marked

Majority of trail is "side-by-side" and grass covered

No gates here, crossing the eastern section of Noe Road

Gem is watching the traffic on I 25

Heading west away from the railroad tracks, the trail becomes sandy

Crossing the northern portion of Spruce Mountain Road

Crossing the western section of Noe Road

One of the stock ponds in the open space area

The southwest portion of the trail becomes a little more
wooded with a mild elevation gain.

Notice, horses have a separate trail here than the hikers and bikers

Crossing the southern section of Spruce Mountain Road

As you ride, check out the various views.

General Information: I don't know how many times I have driven south on I 25 past the Greenland Exit and wondered what it would be like to ride this area. Thanks to Carla from the Perseverance Ranch, LLC, for giving us the opportunity to ride here by allowing us to stay at her ranch on our way south to La Veta.

Spruce Meadows Trail is easy to find, less than a mile west of I 25. The parking lot is massive and would easily accommodate 20+ large trailers. The trail winds through fields of grasses and wildflowers with a minimal elevation gain between the Greenland Open Space and Spruce Mountain. The entrance to the trail is in the southwest corner of the parking lot. Instead of gates to open and close, when a gate is needed, an open space between the fences is created with a large horizontal pole located approximately 10" above the ground. The majority of the trail is a grassy surface that can be slippery at times when riding a horse with shoes. We also noticed that critters (not prairie dogs) have created underground holes that are not visible on the surface that will cause poor footing for your horse. As more and more people ride this trail, I believe the trail will fix itself over time. The trail is wide open, with trees and scrub brush on the southwest portion of the trail. Sunscreen, hats and water are a definite "must have" during the summer months. This would be a great trail for a more experienced beginner rider and/or horse. This would also be a great place to practice "ponying." Shoes are not needed. Open all year, but it would be wise to call ahead for conditions before winter riding.

Notes:

MAP:

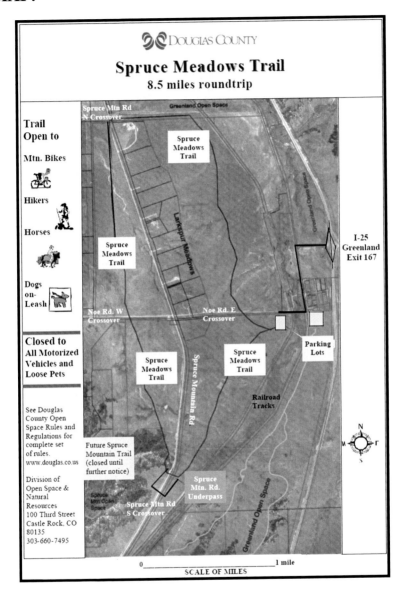

"When I can't ride anymore, I shall keep horses as long as I can hobble along with a bucket and wheelbarrow. When I can't hobble, I shall roll my wheelchair out by the fence of the fields where my horses graze and watch them."
-Monica Dickens

Trail #28

Trail Name:

Greenland Trail (Douglas)

Govt. Organization: Douglas County Open Space (303) 660-7495

Fees: No

Beginning Elevation: 6,950 ft.

Ending Elevation: 7,450 ft.

Trailer Parking: Main parking lot easily accommodates room for 20 or more trailers. There is ample room to maneuver.

Facilities: Restroom, water spigot, hitch rails, kiosk, group picnic shelter accommodating up to 48 people, benches.

Difficulty: Easy - Moderate (trail length and active railroad tracks on west side of trail)

Length of Trail: 10 miles roundtrip

Trail Usage: Horseback riding, hiking, biking
Dogs are permitted on a leash.

Directions: From Denver take I 25 south to the Greenland Exit (#167). Turn west (right) and travel ¼ mile. The road will then jog to the south then continue for ½ mile. The Greenland Trailhead, marked by a large ranch style arch over the entry, will be right in front of you. The trail is also accessible from the south using the New Santa Fe Trail Trailhead at Palmer Lake.

General Information: Even though I ran out of time and was unable to ride this trail, I decided to include the trail in this book because of its close proximity to the Spruce Meadows Trail. The information that I present here will be what I have gathered from the internet as well as from other riders who have ridden the trail.

Trail access is at the southwest of the parking lot. Various portions of the trail consist of crusher fines and natural surfaces. Benches, hitch rails and picnic tables can be found along the 10 miles of trails. The trails wind through rolling grasslands, past ponds and through oak shrub lands and pine forests. The railroad tracks are active with coal trains that run parallel to the west side of the trail. Even though they are not close, the trains are within sight and sound and some horses may spook. You may expect to see elk, mule deer, coyotes, foxes, porcupines, ground squirrels and many varieties of birds. The eastern portion of the Kipps Loop has a gradual 500' elevation gain.

Sunscreen, hats and water are a definite "must have" during the summer months. This would also be a great place to practice "ponying" if you are an experienced rider. Shoes are not needed. Open all year, but it would be wise to call ahead for conditions before winter riding. If wanting to make this a shorter ride, you could have someone drop you off at the Greenland Trail Trailhead and ride to the New Santa Fe Trail Trailhead at Palmer Lake (5 miles), where your trailer could be waiting for you.

Notes:

MAP:

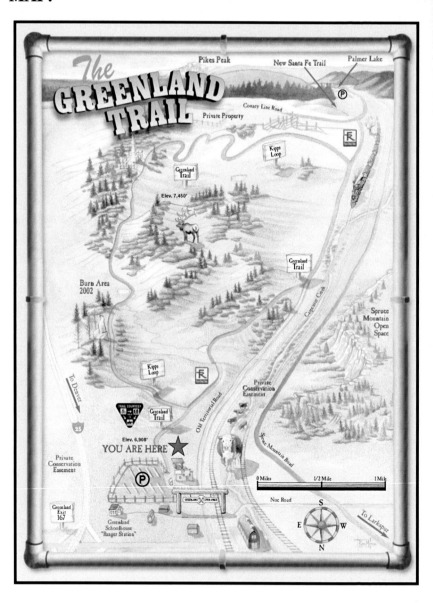

"Like human beings, horses are all individuals with singular personalities, their own virtues and their own faults. We become bound to them for their beauty, their eccentricities, their heart and the love they so often return to us."
-Lana Slaton

The Loss Of A Friend

As I try to put my feelings on paper, words cannot describe the loss I feel for my wonderful companion, Silk. After a horse accident in 1998, I was beginning to think I would never enjoy riding again. The first time I rode Silk, I knew we were right for each other. As an older ranch horse, he put in his years of hard work and I only wanted to do some easy trail riding. He gave me back the confidence I needed and together we had many wonderful rides. I thank my friend and author, Janet, for asking me to go with her on new trails. The saddest day of my life is when I had to make the right decision and say goodbye to my beautiful Palomino in the spring of 2005.

-Carol Chandler

Boulder County Horse Association (BCHA)

The **Boulder County Horse Association** promotes, protects and unifies the equestrian community of Boulder County through education, recreation and legislation.

BCHA serves as an umbrella organization for all horse-related interests in Boulder County. We are a clearinghouse of information and present a united voice for all horse enthusiasts. Our members' equine interests encompass breeding, showing, training, pleasure, ranch activities, and trail riding for competition as well as recreation. BCHA has been incorporated since 1971 as a Colorado non-profit corporation. In 1998 we obtained our 501(c)3 status from the Internal Revenue Service, enabling contributions to the organization to be tax-deductible.

BCHA's newsletter, "The Horse's Mouth," educates our members about horse-related issues. Articles include upcoming events, potential legislative impacts affecting our interests, trail descriptions and useful tidbits about caring for our horses. Seminars and clinics are presented throughout the year. We offer both organized and informal trail rides, which are a great way to learn about local ecology, history and land stewardship.

BCHA promotes the acquisition of open space and parks and supports an interconnected system of multiple-use trails. In 1986 BCHA built and adopted the Doudy Draw Trail near Eldorado Springs for the City of Boulder Open Space & Mountain Parks Department and we have conducted annual maintenance on this trail ever since. We have participated in several National Trails Day projects and our members are active in State and Federal trail-policy planning forums. We are an organizational member of the Boulder Area Trails Coalition and the Colorado Horse Council.

BCHA works with Boulder County to formulate a set of horse-keeping guidelines in the Land Use Code which works for most horse owners, yet enables the County to enforce reasonable regulations should the need arise. BCHA is recognized as a resource for horse-related expertise in land use planning.

BCHA ACTIVITIES

Monthly Board Meetings: First Wednesday of every month. Members and guests welcome.

General Membership Meetings: Annually in February, featuring guest speakers, films, entertainment and topics of interest. Election of the Board of Directors.

Newsletter: Published more-or-less bi-monthly, keeps members informed of local events, trail logs, activities and issues affecting horsemen.

Horse Services Directory: Published approximately every five years, a handy reference for all equestrian services and products in our area.

Clinics and Seminars: Scheduled occasionally, open to the public.

Trail Rides: More-or-less weekly, sharing favorite trails with others.

Trail Building and Maintenance: Co-sponsored with various public land management agencies.

Public Lands Appreciation Day: Opportunity for equestrians to share our world with elected officials and public land managers; usually held in fall.

Horse Lovers' Fling: Fundraising event, usually in the spring, featuring silent auction, booths, entertainment and refreshments.

Publications: Educational material on matters of interest to horse people including "Sharing Trails Safely with Horses," "Colorado's Poisonous Menace: Do you know what your horse is eating?," "Adopt a Trail," "Happy Trails: A collection of essays and trail logs for selected equestrian trails in Boulder County and neighboring areas" and others.

Fun Show: Informal and educational program, usually in early autumn, bringing adults and kids together across all disciplines in a relaxed environment.

H.O.O.F.: Horse Owners' Operation Find, in conjunction with the Boulder County Sheriff's Office, helps reunite horses and owners when a horse is on the loose.

Website: Keeps members and "visitors" informed about upcoming events and issues of interest to the horse community. www.boulderhorse.org.

BCHA can be contacted at info@boulderhorse.org.

PLEASE JOIN US!

316

Suggested Articles to Take On Your Ride

- ❖ EasyBoot(s)
- ❖ Hoof Pick
- ❖ Vet Wrap
- ❖ Small First Aid Kit (people and horse items)
- ❖ Water Bottle(s)
- ❖ Plastic tube(s) (approx ¾ inch in diameter) (If your horse was bitten by a rattlesnake on the nose, these are inserted into the horse's nose to allow your horse to breath)
- ❖ Sun Block
- ❖ Chap Stick
- ❖ Wrap around Sun Glasses (Protects your eyes from the wind and the sun as well as low hanging tree branches)
- ❖ Leather Shoe Laces (I have used laces to replace Chicago screws that have fallen out of my headstall)
- ❖ Cell Phone (Even though cell phone service may not be available in all areas, this is still a good item to carry)
- ❖ Binoculars
- ❖ Compass/GPS unit
- ❖ Map of area with trails if available
- ❖ People Snacks
- ❖ Leatherman Tool (For cutting shoe laces, wire, tighten Chicago screws, etc.)
- ❖ Raincoat (It should be long enough to cover your saddle)
- ❖ Toilet Paper/Tissues
- ❖ Leather gloves (Helps when opening tight barb wire gates)
- ❖ Camera (Not a necessity, but nice to have)
- ❖ Waterproof matches
- ❖ Halter and lead rope (I usually ride with this under my bridle with the end of my lead rope tied to my saddle)
- ❖ Large bells to tie to saddle or breast collar (The noise will let anyone or anything know that you are on the trail)
- ❖ Leg wraps for your horse
- ❖ Pepper Spray
- ❖ Chaps
- ❖ Small flashlight

Suggested Extra Tack and Miscellaneous Items
for Your Horse Trailer

- ❖ Saddle Blanket
- ❖ Bridle
- ❖ Halter
- ❖ Lead Rope
- ❖ Girth Strap
- ❖ Various Horse Brushes
- ❖ Jacket/Sweatshirt/Sweater (In the mountains during the summer, snow is not uncommon)
- ❖ Orange vest for riding during hunting season
- ❖ Leather Work Gloves
- ❖ Winter Gloves
- ❖ Star Nut Wrench (Check to make sure the wrench fits your lug nuts on the horse trailer as well as your towing vehicle)
- ❖ Jack for the horse trailer (The type you drive up on is the easiest)
- ❖ WD40 (I've used this to loosen the lug nuts)
- ❖ Large First Aid Kit
- ❖ Can with lid containing oats (If your horse should get loose, rattling a can with oats might help to get him/her back)
- ❖ Emergency Phone numbers and/or local phone book
- ❖ Couple gallons of water (We use 6 gallon containers)
- ❖ Water Bucket
- ❖ Rake
- ❖ Horse blanket
- ❖ Small wheelbarrow (If camping, this is good for carrying water for your horses as well as the clean-up of manure)
- ❖ Copy of your horse's Brand Inspection
- ❖ Battery operated radio
- ❖ Self contained battery with jumper cables, air compressor and light

Additional Local Information

Local Farriers

John Hunter - (970) 231-7360
Loveland/Ft. Collins

Randy Stephens - (970) 532-5707
Loveland

Ed Bullock – (303) 619-HOOF
Sedalia

Jason Hays – (303) 726-0449
Castle Rock

Jamie Felinczak – (720) 352-1947
Lafayette

Brad Wolfe – (303) 589-8827
Longmont

Jim Fike – (303) 979-0890
Morrison

Michael J McMillan – (720) 4094
Arvada

Local Veterinarians

Susan J. Williams, DVM
(970) 461-2061

Laporte Animal Clinic & Supply
(970) 490-1999

Colorado State University-Veterinary
(970) 221-4535

Boulder Valley Veterinary Clinic
(303) 440-8440

Alpine Equine Services
(303) 443-6506

Local Feed & Tack Stores

Ranch-Way Feeds
Ft. Collins, CO
(970) 482-1662

Poudre Pet & Feed Supply
Ft. Collins, CO
(970) 484-2461 or (970) 225-1255

Jax Farm & Ranch
Ft. Collins, CO
(970) 484-2221

287 Supply
Ft. Collins, CO
(970) 493-7322

Westside Feed
Loveland, CO
(970) 622-8658

Happy Horse Tack & Saddle Shop
Ft. Collins, CO
(970) 484-4199

Nightwinds Tack Shop, Inc.
Berthoud, CO
(970) 532-2463

Vetline
Ft. Collins, CO
(970) 484-1900

Additional Local Information
(Continued)

Local Feed & Tack Stores

Murdoch's Ranch & Supply
Littleton, CO
(303) 791-7800

Murdoch's Ranch & Supply
Longmont, CO
(303) 682-5111

Hygiene Feed & Supply
Hygiene, CO
(303) 776-4757

Lafayette Feed & Grain
Lafayette, CO
(303) 665-5055

Country Corner Feed & Pet, LLC
Greeley, CO
(970) 351-0868

Johnstown Feed & Seed, Inc
Johnstown, CO
(970) 587-4681

Brighton Feed & Saddlery
Brighton, CO
(303) 659-0721

Boulder Horse & Rider
Boulder, CO
(303) 440-3466

Losson's Pony Express
Golden, CO
(303) 274-6220

Spirit Horse Saddlery
Elizabeth, CO
(303) 646-1049

West Bros. Inc.
Arvada, CO
(303) 403-0288

J & T Country Feeds, Inc.
Greeley, CO
(970) 378-0240

Pine Country Feed
Pine, CO
(303) 838-5186

Frank's Feed & Supply
Elizabeth, CO
(303) 646-4730

Rampart Feed & Pet Supply
Castle Rock, CO
(303) 688-7360

Stockyards
Commerce City, CO
(303) 287-8081

Golden Mill
Golden, CO
(303) 279-1151

Parker Feed
Parker, CO
(303) 841-3955

Discount Horse Supply
Parker, CO
(303) 841-9128

Horse And Hound
Franktown, CO
(303) 694-0411

Additional Local Information
(Continued)

Bed & Breakfast with horse facilities

Kenlyn Stables
1000 Salida Street
Aurora, CO 80011
(303) 364-9556; cellular phone – (303)807-0062

Short Term Overnight Boarding

Falcon Creek Farm, LLC
Quality Boarding & Lessons
13025 Falcon Hwy Falcon, Colorado 80831
Leslie Laing (719) 439-6605

Sun Pony Ranch
WCR1
Berthoud, Co
(970) 532-4040

Calico Stables
3204 South County Road 21
Loveland, Co
(970) 219-6060

Medicine Wind Ranch
11992 WCR 78
Eaton, CO
(970) 443-1149

Colorado Division of Wildlife

DOW Headquarters
6060 Broadway
Denver, Co 80216
(303) 297-1192

Ft. Collins Service Center
317 W. Prospect
Ft. Collins, Co 80536
(970) 472-4300

Certified Weed-Free Hay or Cubes

Suppliers

Ranch-Way Feeds
546 Willow
Ft. Collins, Co
(970) 493-7322

Northern Colorado Feeder Supply
359 Linden
Ft. Collins, Co
(970) 482-7303

Poudre Pet & Feed Supply
6204 S. College
Ft. Collins, Co
(970) 225-1255

287 Supply
120 N. Hwy 287
Ft. Collins, Co
(970) 493-7322

Weed-Free Hay Producers are listed by:

Colorado Department of Agriculture
Division of Plant Industry
Lakewood, Co 80215
(303)239-4149
www.ag.state.co.us/dpi
Click weed-free forage

Acknowledgements

Foolishly, I believed that the experiences of writing the 2nd book would be about the same as the 1st. Was I wrong!! Each trail that I rode with my horse "Gem" made me a better rider and exposed my horse to new trail experiences. I would think that the last trail was the most beautiful, but lo and behold, the next trail I rode was even better. I thank God for making Colorado so beautiful and versatile with so many horse trails being available to me to explore. To my riding partners and friends: Mary and her horse "Sonny", Carol and her horse "Silk", Hugh and his horse "Traveler", Heather and her horse "George", Jane and her horse "Brass", a big thank you for all of the miles we have ridden together. Yet again, without the encouragement that my husband Will gave me along the way, this second book would not be possible. His suggestions and proof reading continues to be extremely appreciated and valued. I appreciated his patience with me when I was away so many times from home. To my family; my daughter, mother, sister and yes even my brothers, for listening to me and talking me through the rough spots, a big "Thank You." To my farrier, John Hunter, thank you again for keeping my horse well shod.

I hope this book will lead you and your horse to many more memorable rides. Keep a lookout for the next book in the series due out in the Fall of 2006:

Horse Trails of "Colorful" Colorado

Southern Colorado–Book 3

(Contains trails from Las Animas, Huerfano, Otero, Bent, Pueblo, El Paso, Custer, Fremont, Saguache & nearby counties)

Check out the website for upcoming events at
www.horsebacktrails.com

Contact me with feedback at **horsebacktrails@yahoo.com**

Or

Ride The Western Trails Publications
2204 Eagle Drive
Loveland, Colorado 80537

NOTES

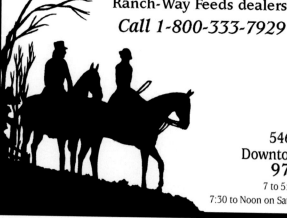

Scott Murdock Trailer Sales
Loveland and Grand Junction, CO
Contact us @ (800) 688-8757 or
e-mail at olemurdock@aol.com

327

I personally own a set of the 5'panels that I use when camping with my horse. After the initial "test" setup, the assembly has become extremely easy and quick, whether setting it up or tearing it down. I am delighted that the panels are extremely lightweight, yet durable enough for my horse's security. Their compact size allows me to easily maneuver them on my own. If you are looking for something heavier than electric wire fencing yet lighter than metal panels, these are for you!!   - Janet St. Jacques

The Card Corral

Custom Embroidery and Digitizing

EMBROIDERY SHOP
Linda Sullivan - Owner

970-667-0253
Fax 970-613-0751

3705 Carbondale St.
Loveland, CO 80538

West Bros. Inc.

Handmade Saddles and Tack
Complete Saddle Shop
High Quality Cowboy Gear
Complete Line of Livestock Feed
Quality Ranch Horses for Sale
7040 Indiana St. Arvada, Colorado 80007

(303) 403-0288   (303) 403-0901 Fax

The Card Corral

LARSON LABORATORIES, INC.

VETLINE

Kenneth A. Larson, DVM, Ph.D.

425 John Deere Road • Fort Collins, Colorado 80524

1-800-962-4554 • (970) 484-1900 • Fax: (970) 484-7666

HORSESHOEING
Edward W. Bullock

P.O. Box 708
Sedalia, CO 80135
303-619-HOOF

The Card Corral

HAYS HORSESHOEING
Jason Hays

Graduate of Heartland Horseshoeing School

1530 Royal Troon Dr
Castle Rock, CO 80104

(303) 726-0449

Correct Shoeing for Balance & Performance

Reliable, Professional Service

Purina Mills, Inc.

HYGIENE FEED & SUPPLY
Old fashioned friendly service!

P.O. Box 235
7455 Hygiene Road
Hygiene, Colorado 80533
303-776-4757

Jeanne & Greg Jackson

The Card Corral

The Card Corral

At last there's a ma[g]
places only a horse

*If you love to ride where the only signpost
is a hoofprint...*

*If you look forward to the adventure beyond
each bend of the trail...*

*If you savor the time spent with a good
horse and good companions...*

Welcome to
The Trail Rider!

The Trail Rider is the colorful, informative
bimonthly magazine that shows you how
and where to enjoy trail and recreational
riding to its fullest.

You'll get recommendations on destinations,
previews of great trail rides, guidance for
effective horse care and training, tips for
buying tack and equipment,
and more!

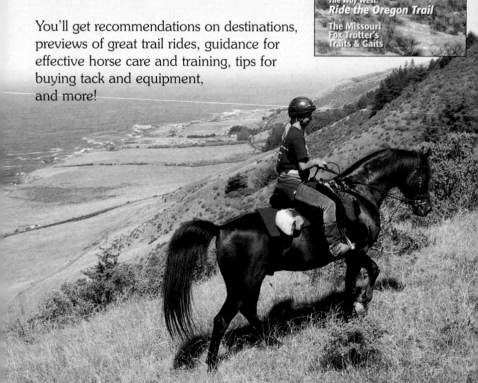

...ine that takes you
...n go!

You'll discover
WHERE...

Each issue takes you to spectacular trails and top-notch horse camps and lodges across the country with first-person reviews and personal impressions. You'll read about upcoming trail rides, backcountry trips, cowboy roundups and memorable day rides.

You'll find out
HOW...

The Trail Rider brings you authoritative information for fortifying your horse's health and maintaining his soundness and stamina.

And The Trail Rider is a valuable learning experience. Top trainers regularly share lesson plans to prepare your horse for the demands and distractions of the trail.

You'll learn
WHAT...

The Trail Rider is your hitching post for honest assessments of gear and tack. You'll read instructive articles on selecting everything from hoof boots and haynets to hitches and trailers.

Also, you'll get vital insights for outfitting. You'll be briefed on such topics as how to fit the gear to the trip, how to break in tack and what to pack for emergencies.

PLUS, you'll enjoy a herd of other regular features including...

■ **Trailblazers.** Interviews with top trekkers, trainers and innovators who are advancing the sport of trail riding and adding to our understanding of our horses.

■ **Hot on the Trail.** Late-breaking news of rides, special offers from top facilities, changing state regulations, and upoming expos.

■ **Breed Showcase.** In-depth looks at different breeds with answers to the questions a prospective buyer should ask.

Because you ride for miles, you're invited to preview the one magazine that can go the distance!

Send for your FREE preview issue of *The Trail Rider* today